KT-503-765

The
FRIENDSHIP
BOOK

of Francis Gay

D. C. THOMSON & CO., LTD.
London   Glasgow   Manchester   Dundee

A Thought
For Each Day
In 2000

A TIME of new beginnings
     For all of us to share,
A time of looking forward
     For people, everywhere.
A time to cherish hopes and dreams,
     To search for love and joy,
And make a peaceful future
     Which nothing can destroy.

And though this new millennium
     Brings changes for us all,
We still can count our blessings,
     Some great, and others small.
Then stepping forward through the years
     With joyful expectations,
We'll build a better, fairer world
     And share the celebrations!

January

IN times gone by watch night services were common and people went to their local church on New Year's Eve to give thanks for the departing year and to rejoice in the coming of a new one. As the clock reached midnight, bells rang out all over the country.

This year we welcome not only a new year, but a new millennium, with all its hopes and aspirations.

For hope shall brighten days to come,
And memory gild the past!
Bells ring out the old and bad —
Ring in the new and good.

In the words of St Paul: "Old things are passed away; behold, all things are become new". May this New Year and this new millennium be all you hope it will be.

GOD is our refuge and strength, a very present help in trouble. Therefore will not we fear, though the earth be removed, and though the mountains be carried into the midst of the sea.

Psalms 46:1-2

MONDAY—JANUARY 3.

*D*ON'T be afraid of the year,
   Don't be afraid to begin,
Just open your mind and open your heart,
   Let love and hope enter in.
Don't be afraid to let go,
   Saying "Goodbye" to the past,
Seek for a rainbow and search for a star
   And keep a few dreams, hold them fast.
Don't be afraid to be glad,
   Tears are not only for sorrow,
Welcome the future and step through the year —
   Look for the sunshine tomorrow.

          Iris Hesselden.

TUESDAY—JANUARY 4.

MOTHER TERESA will be remembered as the tiny nun with love and compassion in her eyes as she held tiny babies in her arms, and who worked until the end of her life helping the poorest people in India. I particularly like these thoughtful words of hers:

"Everybody has something good inside them. Some hide it, some neglect it, but it is there."

WEDNESDAY—JANUARY 5.

IT is good to know that other cultures have inspiring and thought-provoking proverbs, as we have. Here are two — the first is Nigerian, the second comes from Tonga, the Friendly Islands:

"Hold a true friend with both your hands";
"Friendship is a furrow in the sand."

THE FRIENDSHIP BOOK

<u>THURSDAY—JANUARY 6.</u>

THE 11-year-old daughter of our friend Jean was once showing me her school report. She hadn't been awarded top marks for anything but the report ended with these words: "Susan has the ability to work hard and to remain cheerful. This makes her a valuable member of her class. She should do well."

Many of Susan's friends had higher marks, so Susan does not think of herself as clever. But I don't agree. Hard work *and* cheerfulness — what a clever combination!

<u>FRIDAY—JANUARY 7.</u>

IT was a cold, dismal January morning, not at all the sort of weather to encourage me to go outside — until the telephone rang. It was our friends Eric and Joyce with an invitation to go to their house for lunch that day.

"I've already prepared enough for two extra guests in the hope that you can come and join us," said Joyce who is an excellent cook. You may be sure that it only took the Lady of the House and me a couple of seconds to accept the invitation.

What a pleasant time we had together that day as we turned our backs on the dreary weather outside. As Joyce remarked, "We all need to give ourselves a treat to help us along in January."

And do you know, as we walked home, the weather didn't feel nearly as cold as it had when we started out!

SATURDAY—JANUARY 8.

SOME time ago there was an invitation posted on a board outside Burley-in-Wharfedale Methodist Church in West Yorkshire. It said: "Come In For A Faith Lift!"

There are other types of faith lifts, apart from this important reminder. One example is the way we feel after meeting a friendly face when we've been feeling a little bruised by the ups and downs of life. A second example is an unexpected kindness or courtesy received, while a third is an unexpected letter from a friend.

All these can be called faith lifts, for they remind us of the good and simple things of life, so important in daily living.

SUNDAY—JANUARY 9.

FOR there is one God, and one mediator between God and men, the man Christ Jesus.

Timothy I 2:5

MONDAY—JANUARY 10.

MAKE this day a happy day,
Make it work for you.
Put the zest and joy of life
In all you say and do.
Love and laugh, be positive,
Enthusiastic, bright.
Say no to all that's negative —
Soon all will turn out right.

Kathleen Gillum.

TUESDAY—JANUARY 11.

IAN BRADLEY was a small boy during the Depression of the 1930s. His father was a miner who lived in one of the small villages near Barnsley in Yorkshire. There was no money for toys, so Ian learned how to make his own, painstakingly carving them from wood with his pocket knife.

Ian became a miner, too. After he retired, he went into his garden shed and spent hours carving ornaments — things of beauty for his own home, and for his friends. He also went regularly to the local hospice to cheer the patients by showing them what can be achieved with a small piece of wood and a penknife.

Ian's hobby obviously gave him a great deal of happiness. "I would never have had all this pleasure if money had not been so scarce when I was a boy," he said. He never looked back to those times of hardship with regrets — only thanks.

WEDNESDAY—JANUARY 12.

DO you sometimes say in a dismissive way — "Not for me! I can't imagine why he or she wants to do that, go there, buy, read or wear that."

The Lady of the House caught me doing this the other day, and quoted these words of Konrad Adenauer: "We all live under the same sky, but we don't all have the same horizons."

How true! And isn't it a very good thing that we don't?

SILVER
WEBBING

THURSDAY—JANUARY 13.

WE all admire climbers who reach the top of Mount Everest. To do so takes strength, stamina and determination far beyond most of us.

Is it right, though, to speak of "conquering" Everest? Jim Crumley, the Scottish writer and climber, does not think so. He says: "Man has done no such thing; he has been permitted to climb by the grace of the mountain."

He recalls how Tenzing, the Sherpa who accompanied the first party to the summit, prayed for forgiveness every time he wielded his ice axe. He felt — not pride — but anguish on the historic ascent. His people respect the mountain, and feel they have a bond with it.

"We look at Everest," he said, "and we see ourselves. We are the blood, the mountain is the bone."

I am glad there are Western climbers, too, men like Jim Crumley, who share something of Tenzing's humility.

FRIDAY—JANUARY 14.

THE Lady of the House and I were asked to choose a favourite line from a prayer. By coincidence we both chose lines written by a 17th-century nun. Mine was: "Teach me the glorious lesson that occasionally I may be mistaken". The Lady of the House chose: "Make me thoughtful but not moody, helpful but not bossy."

What's your favourite prayer quote?

SATURDAY—JANUARY 15.

"**D**O you know, Francis," announced our young friend Paula, "I'm really looking forward to Easter." I laughingly reminded her it was only mid-January.

"Yes, I know," she replied, "but the thought of daffodils, lambs and a holiday will keep me going through the rest of the Winter."

I had to agree it was indeed a lovely thought and well worth keeping in mind. After she left, I considered how we all need something to look forward to. It needn't be anything expensive — perhaps something as simple as the delights of savouring a seat by the fire with a good book after a hard day's work; the sight of the first snowdrop; or even the first chocolate in an unopened box!

If we can nourish cheerful thoughts and keep on looking ahead with optimism, then we can easily face all these dark days of Winter.

SUNDAY—JANUARY 16.

I WILL not leave you comfortless: I will come to you.

John 14:18

MONDAY—JANUARY 17.

I FEEL sure we can each describe what we mean by a home, but I don't think we can improve on the definition by that delightful character Ratty in Kenneth Grahame's "Wind In The Willows":

"Light, warmth, love — a home".

THE FRIENDSHIP BOOK

TUESDAY—JANUARY 18.

O N the wall of the main United States Post Office in Washington is this inscription:

Messenger of Sympathy and Love
Servant of Parted Friends
Consoler of the Lonely
Bond of the Scattered Family
Enlarger of the Common Life
Carrier of News and Knowledge
Instrument of Trade and Industry
Promoter of Mutual Acquaintance
Of Peace and Good Will.

This is the real meaning of a letter — so often a completely unexpected message to brighten the day, isn't it?

WEDNESDAY—JANUARY 19.

H ERE is one of Dr William Barclay's prayers; lovely thoughts for the beginning of a new day:

"O God, as I go out to life and work today,
I thank you for the world's beauty:
For the light of the sun;
For the wind on my face;
For the colour of the flowers;
and for all glimpses of lovely things.
I thank you for life's gracious things:
For friendship's help;
For kinship's strength;
For love's wonder."

THURSDAY—JANUARY 20.

THE composer Beethoven was not exactly renowned for his social graces. When he became deaf at the age of 30, conversation became difficult, even embarrassing. Then, suddenly, the son of one of his friends died in an accident. What could he do or say in such tragic circumstances?

He went round to see his friend. There were no words of comfort he felt able to offer, but there was a piano in the room — and Beethoven went straight across to it.

For the next half-hour or so he poured out his feelings of grief in the most expressive way he knew. And then he left in his usual abrupt manner.

Later, his friend remarked that during his time of anguish, Beethoven's visit had truly been a priceless gift. When words fail us, for whatever reason, we should remember that other channels of communication are open, if only we can learn to find them.

FRIDAY—JANUARY 21.

ONE of our neighbours makes her own greetings cards to send to friends and family. She sometimes finds a particular message to include which makes the card just that much more special. Here is one to share with you:

"Love joins our present
   with the past
  and the future."
     Khalil Gibran.

AFTER EIGHT . . .

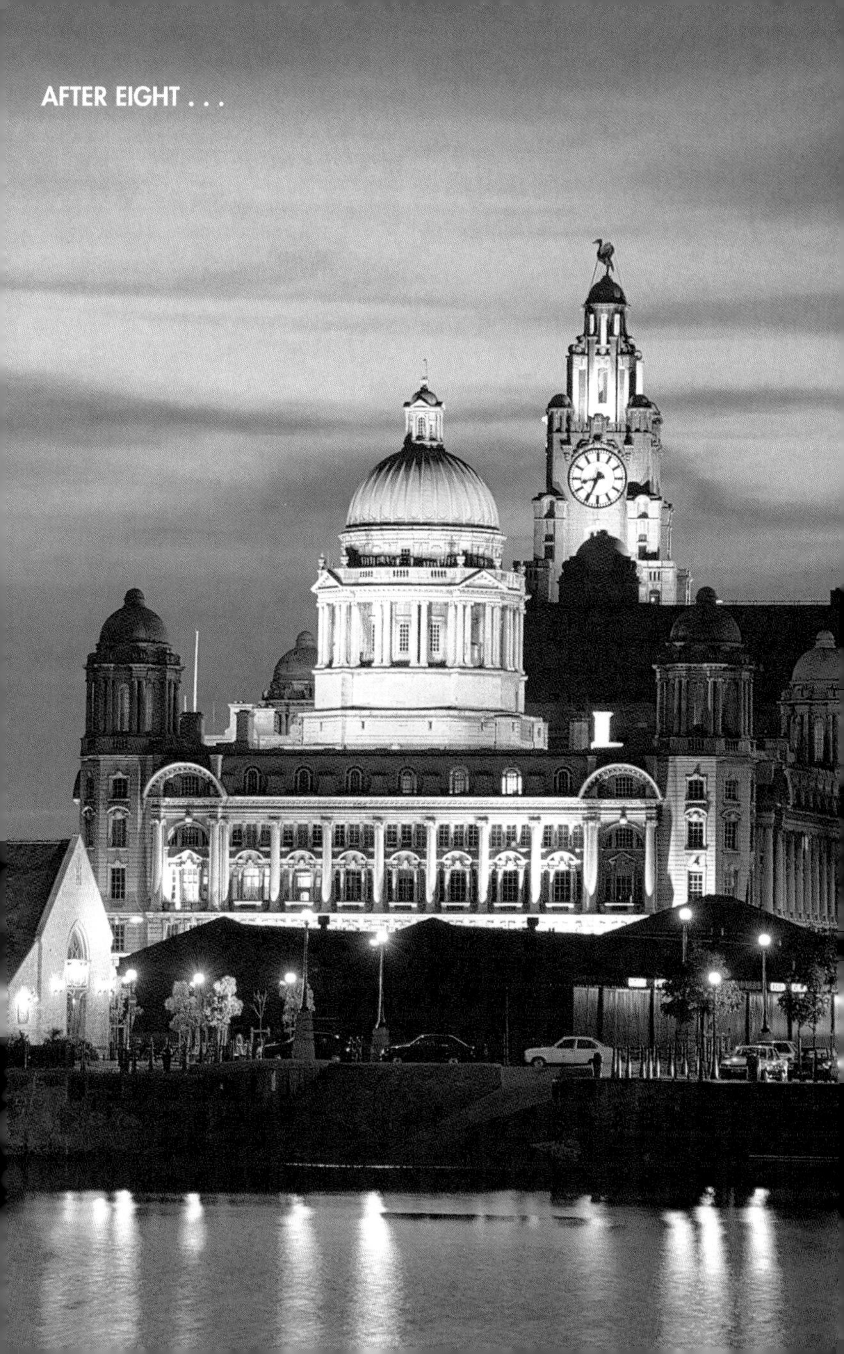

SATURDAY—JANUARY 22.

IT'S a joy to walk along a river bank — that is, until you want to get to the other side and then a bridge seems a long way away! That's when we are thankful for the stepping stones set firmly into the riverbed by our ancestors many years ago. Thus we can cross the water today, taking one careful step at a time.

Isn't that just like life? Problems come and pressure mounts but if we take just one step at a time, pausing only to balance before taking the next, we will overcome all obstacles and eventually win through.

It is taking the next careful step that is most important, the one that counts for the future.

SUNDAY—JANUARY 23.

FOR thine is the kingdom, and the power, and the glory, for ever. Amen.

Matthew 6:13

MONDAY—JANUARY 24.

SURPRISING things can happen to anyone who, when a disagreeable or discouraged thought comes into his or her mind, just has the sense to remember in time to push it out by putting in a positive and determinedly courageous one. These two things cannot occupy the same space.

As Frances Hodgson Burnett wrote in "The Secret Garden": "Where you tend a rose, my lad, a thistle cannot grow."

TUESDAY—JANUARY 25.

MISS BROWN still lives in exactly the same flat where she was born, over her parents' greengrocer's shop.

When she was a child she loved to look from an upstairs window to the house on the opposite side of the road, with its huge garden and rhododendron-lined driveway, where a well-to-do solicitor lived. As she got older, she began to help in the shop and one of her jobs was to deliver orders to the house across the road. So began a friendship between the elderly gentleman and the young messenger. In one conversation, Miss Brown confided that it gave her great pleasure to be able to see that garden from her window.

One day the solicitor said, "You need never fear you will lose your lovely view, my dear. My land will never be built on. When I am gone I have arranged that it will be given to the people of this town as a place of recreation, forever."

Miss Brown can still enjoy her view today and look across to the river beyond — and all because of the vision and kindness of one man.

WEDNESDAY—JANUARY 26.

"WHILE there's tea there's hope," says a character in Pinero's play, "The Second Mrs Tanqueray". It's true, isn't it? Many a problem has been solved over a cup of tea, and I suppose most of us at some time have set down our cup and risen with a lighter heart.

Here's to a good pot of tea!

THURSDAY—JANUARY 27.

EVERY day, Dundee businessman William Reid would check his watch by the time on a nearby church clock. "Wouldn't it be wonderful," he thought, "if instead of a simple chime, that steeple had a whole carillon of bells?"

And so in 1913, he bequeathed £3000 to provide, after his death, a peal of bells at St Andrew's Church in memory of his sister, Jane. They were duly made and installed in 1950, by a London firm of bellfounders who'd been in existence in Whitechapel since the 16th century.

And ever since, they've been ringing out the well-loved hymn tunes in welcome. A wonderful way to preserve someone's memory, wouldn't you agree?

FRIDAY—JANUARY 28.

A KEEN bird-watcher friend, Helen, once went on a guided walk entitled "Good Morning With The Birds." It meant getting up at four o'clock in the morning! Off she went with her binoculars, notebook and pencils, and later returned full of enthusiasm for what she had seen and heard.

I loved the words she had written on the cover of her notebook:

The dawn shall be glad
with the song of birds,
and the stir of fluttering wings;
Surely the joy of life is found
in simple tender things.

SATURDAY—JANUARY 29.

I ONCE asked a doctor, "Don't you sometimes get discouraged seeing sick people every day?"

"Never," he answered. "They cheer me up! The sickest people are often the bravest. They make me feel humble — and proud of the privilege to serve them."

SUNDAY—JANUARY 30.

IN my Father's house are many mansions: if it were not so, I would have told you. I go to prepare a place for you.

John 14: 2

MONDAY—JANUARY 31.

AN ancient Corinthian seems to keep on appearing in articles and books. His name is Sisyphus.

Never heard of him? Well, neither had I until I came across him in one of Angus MacVicar's autobiographical works, and soon afterwards he was mentioned in John Prebble's "Scotland", then later in Howard Spring's writings. We are now old acquaintances, you might say.

This mythical character was condemned by underworld gods to push a huge boulder uphill. Whenever Sisyphus almost reached the summit, it rolled down to the foot again. Never-ending effort — that was Sisyphus's lot.

But he's become the messenger for all tenacious folk. Keep on trying, again and again, even when things seem to be continually slipping downhill.

February

TUESDAY—FEBRUARY 1.

WHEN we feel that we have perhaps bitten off more than we can chew, and feel inadequate, sure that our best is not good enough, isn't it cheering and heartening to hear someone say with a smile, "You're getting there!" Or maybe they will say, "That is very good!" or "You are managing fine!"

Are you a grand praiser? I try to be and hope you do, too!

WEDNESDAY—FEBRUARY 2.

HOW grateful I am for our public libraries with their well-stocked shelves of books. I like to choose at least three books each week — one to stretch my mind, one to bring a relaxing end to my day plus one for pure enjoyment.

Terry Waite, when a hostage, wrote: "Good food, good books and good walks are my idea of heaven," while Thomas à Kempis wrote: "I have sought for rest everywhere. But I have found it nowhere except in a corner with a book."

As the saying goes — "You are never alone with a good book". I'll second that and propose a toast to the many pleasures which a good book provides.

THURSDAY—FEBRUARY 3.

LET me share with you today these words written by George Herbert, a 17th-century poet and country clergyman, who in the last years of his short life lived at Bemerton, near Salisbury:

"God oft hath a great share in a little house".

His ten words don't take long to read, but how wise they are, don't you think?

FRIDAY—FEBRUARY 4.

I HAVE to admit it — February has never been my favourite month. With the excitement of Christmas gone, and the full beauty of Spring yet to come, it sometimes seems that the only distinctive thing about February is in living up to its nickname — "February fill-dyke".

And yet, leafing through an old almanac, I was amazed to discover just what a full month February actually is. For example, it contains more than a dozen saints' days, not forgetting St Valentine's Day! Even the coldest grey Winter's day has been brightened by the arrival of a Valentine card.

Other February traditions are interesting. Now, did you know that snowdrops in the house are said to cleanse and purify it? And if the first lamb you see is facing towards you, you'll have good luck, it is said.

There's far more to look out for in February than I ever realised!

NATURE'S SCULPTURE

SATURDAY—FEBRUARY 5.

I HAVE had many a laugh when browsing through old autograph albums. There is often many a witty or wise saying to be found beside each signature. I was interested to come across a collection of "Poetry Thoughts And Merry Jests" made by Beryl Peters, which contained this extract taken from an autograph album, written in 1911:

> *What? Lost your temper, did you?*
>   *Well, dear, I would not mind it,*
> *It is not such a dreadful loss —*
>   *Pray do not try to find it!*

Very wise advice, surely.

SUNDAY—FEBRUARY 6.

MY tabernacle also shall be with them: yea, I will be their God, and they shall be my people.

Ezekiel 37:27

MONDAY—FEBRUARY 7.

> *WHERE is the road to Happiness?*
>   *It's somewhere on Life's route,*
> *And the kind of destination*
>   *That is worthy of pursuit.*
> *With Optimism acting*
>   *As a guide, the map's inclined*
> *To show the road to Happiness*
>   *Is not so hard to find.*

J. M. Robertson.

TUESDAY—FEBRUARY 8.

LITTLE Lucy had been kept indoors with a heavy cold, and in an effort to keep her amused, her mother had allowed her to flick through the family photograph albums. Leafing through, Lucy paused at a picture of a small girl, clad in sun-bonnet and smock, playing on a beach.

"Who's that?" she asked, puzzled.

"It's me!" replied her mother.

"You?" said Lucy in indignant disbelief. "But it can't be you — you're a mummy!"

Now Lucy is young, and we can smile at her words but, in a way, her mistake is one which we can all make. We get so used to seeing people only as they appear to us now, that we often forget they were younger once, with a life perhaps quite different from the one they now lead. So next time we're tempted to base our opinions only on outward appearance, let's remember Lucy!

WEDNESDAY—FEBRUARY 9.

TODAY'S THE DAY!

TAKE the chance that comes today,
Tomorrow may not do!
Yesterday is in the past,
Today is bright and new.
Don't let opportunity
Start to fade away,
Do the very things you know
Are wiser done today!

Elizabeth Gozney.

THURSDAY—FEBRUARY 10.

WHAT is a family? Well, there are many definitions but this is one which I particularly like:

"A family is people who care when you're sad,
Who love you no matter what,
Who share your triumphs,
Who don't expect you to be perfect,
Just growing with honesty
In your own direction."

FRIDAY—FEBRUARY 11.

SIR WALTER SCOTT wrote of that well-loved writer Jane Austen, born in Steventon parsonage in Hampshire in 1775:

"That young lady has a talent for describing the involvements, and feelings and characters of ordinary life, which is to me the most wonderful I ever met."

Perhaps that is why Jane's novels have been reprinted so many times, serialised on radio, and dramatised in films and on television. However, success did not come easily to Jane; she could not find a publisher for her early work. One refused to read the novel, which 15 years later was to appear under the title "Pride And Prejudice". Another was accepted, only to lie forgotten in a drawer for several years.

When success eludes our grasp, perhaps we should remember the words of Winston Churchill: — "Ride at the fence in faith and good cheer; you will clear it".

SATURDAY—FEBRUARY 12.

MILES divide us from our minister friend Bob these days, but we are still as good friends as we were when he was a young teacher living near to us.

Bob moved recently to another church and we were invited to his induction service. It was a very large church, the bells were ringing and it was full to the great oak door with his friends, all praying and wishing him well.

At the reception afterwards he made a short speech telling us how amazed and how happy he was to see so many gathered together.

"I have just finished tracing my family tree," he said, "and now I am going to start a Friendship Tree! You will all be there on its spreading branches, loved and remembered." What a wonderful idea!

The Lady of the House has started one, too, and we are surprised to find how many kind and loving friends we have. Why not adopt this idea?

SUNDAY—FEBRUARY 13.

AND God saw every thing that he had made, and, behold, it was very good.

Genesis 1: 31

MONDAY—FEBRUARY 14.

TIME to talk, time to listen — two priceless gifts we can give to the lonely. Do you have them to give? Think about it and you might well find that you do!

TUESDAY—FEBRUARY 15.

THE Rev. Wilbert Vere Awdry gave pleasure to countless children with his little books about Thomas The Tank Engine and his friends. Once he was asked why clergymen like him are often so fascinated by steam engines.

He thought for a moment and then replied, "Because both parties are still the best means of getting people to their destination!"

WEDNESDAY—FEBRUARY 16.

IT was good to read that staff working for one of our leading supermarket chains decided that help for disabled customers should be a priority.

The stores had already provided extra-wide parking spaces near the entrance and broader checkouts to accommodate wheelchairs, but the staff felt more could be done. They organised voluntary awareness workshops so they could learn about the needs of disabled shoppers, and worked closely with both the Royal National Institute for the Blind and the Royal National Institute for Deaf People. Some were so keen they volunteered to learn sign language.

Those who complete the course are given a "Helping Hands" badge for their uniform — two linked hands, which they wear with pride, ready to do their utmost to fulfil their own promise of "an equal level of service for everyone".

It is a real step forward and one that deserves the highest praise.

THURSDAY—FEBRUARY 17.

*I*F there is righteousness in the heart
    There will be beauty in the character.
If there is beauty in the character
    There will be harmony in the home.
If there is harmony in the home
    There will be order in the nation.
When there is order in each nation,
    There will be peace in the world.

FRIDAY—FEBRUARY 18.

OUR friend Janet keeps one of those wipeable boards on her kitchen wall. She uses it to write a verse or a thought that has meant something special to her, and she calls it her "motto for the week". She says that by putting it in a place where she spends lots of time, it is a constant reminder to her. Here is an example:

A house is built of logs and stone,
Of tiles and post and piers;
A home is built of loving deeds
That stand a thousand years.   (Victor Hugo)

At the bottom of Janet's board, however, is a sentence that must have impressed her a great deal for it has been there as long as I can remember:

"Each day is a new opportunity to correct the mistakes of yesterday and to deal with the challenges that face us today".

                    (Father Jerome Le Doux)

What better motto could any one of us have?

SATURDAY—FEBRUARY 19.

HELEN KELLER, that brave and remarkable lady, once wrote that when one door to happiness closes, another opens, but often we stand looking so long at the closed door we don't notice the one that has opened.

SUNDAY—FEBRUARY 20.

THE night is far spent, the day is at hand: let us therefore cast off the works of darkness, and let us put on the armour of light.

Romans 13:12

MONDAY—FEBRUARY 21.

HOW the old ideas about behaviour still tend to be kept in mind — for example, boys are often expected to be brave and not to cry. Perhaps we feel embarrassed if a man cries. Why? In the same way, we often say how brave a person is when they hold back tears at a time of great sorrow.

But crying is a form of release given to us for times of grief and great stress, and it is an emotion which can help others. I am reminded of a wonderful story I once heard.

A little girl came home after playing with a friend. "Mummy," she said, "Debbie is very unhappy because her kitten has died. But I helped her when she cried."

"That's good," said her mother. "Did you tell her not to cry any more?"

"Oh, no," came the reply, "I cried with her."

TUESDAY—FEBRUARY 22.

IN Perthshire stands an old church, by the name of Logiebride. Long unused, it suffers the fate of many an ancient burial ground — some stones have collapsed and many inscriptions are illegible.

I once attempted to read the names recorded but it was impossible to make them all out. However one stone caught my attention. At its base were the easily-read words: "I am The Resurrection and The life".

No matter the passage of time this message will never fade.

WEDNESDAY—FEBRUARY 23.

OUR friend Alice was telling us that she once asked her brother, a jeweller, to explain the differences between different sorts of pearls.

Apparently, artificial pearls are entirely man-made and of little value. Cultured pearls, on the other hand, are formed when a little bit of grit is placed into the shell. This causes irritation and makes the oyster respond by producing a secretion which surrounds the foreign body, eventually forming a cultivated pearl.

On the other hand, a real pearl, often of great value, is created when some mishap befalls the oyster, quite independent of man's interference. A swelling develops in the shell, and a protective covering is produced, which later forms a pearl.

Is there not a lesson to be learned here? Whatever the original cause of a problem, start growing a pearl.

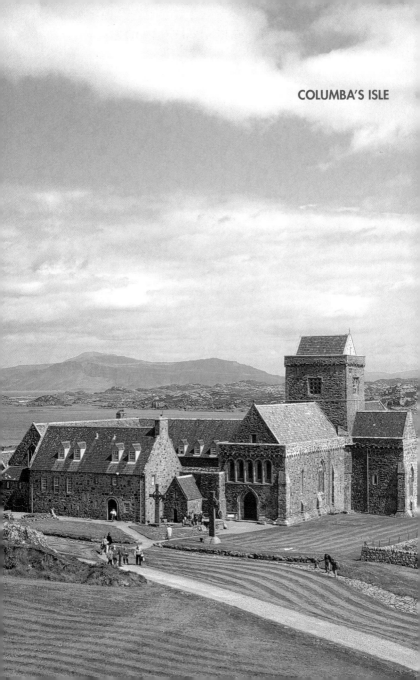

THURSDAY—FEBRUARY 24.

OUR friend Dora has been very busy knitting six-inch woollen squares. It was quite an effort for her, as she is well over 80, her sight is poor and she suffers from stiff joints.

Then the ladies of the Women's Fellowship brought round to Dora's house a large shawl which one of them had crafted from Dora's squares.

"I never imagined," she exclaimed, "that my little pieces of knitting could be made into such a lovely shawl!"

Even our apparently smallest efforts can count in the most surprising ways.

FRIDAY—FEBRUARY 25.

IBSEN, the Norwegian playwright, the author of such masterpieces as "Peer Gynt", was a great success in his lifetime, and no doubt this brought him a good standard of living. Besides his dramatic writing skills, he was also something of a philosopher and I think his ideas about money are most revealing:

"Money may be the husk of many things, but not the kernel. It brings you food, but not appetite; medicine, but not health; acquaintances, but not friends; servants, but not loyalty; days of joy, but not peace or happiness".

SATURDAY—FEBRUARY 26.

THE world is full of wonderful things — don't miss them as you hurry by!

SUNDAY—FEBRUARY 27.

AND thou shalt love the Lord thy God with all thy heart, and with all thy soul, and with all thy mind, and with all thy strength: this is the first commandment.

Mark 12:30

MONDAY—FEBRUARY 28.

WELL, I've heard some stay-young health tips in my time, but what about this one? "Want to stay younger looking? Then join a choir. People who sing exercise their facial muscles, preventing wrinkles."

Now, maybe we're not unduly worried about wrinkles but it did make me think and assess the value of singing in general. To start with, you cannot remain angry with someone while singing; it can stop you feeling lonely, and many of us do get lonely at times; it can raise the spirits on a rainy day, so sing along with the radio! The words don't matter, but the important thing is just to join in and sing, and you'll be surprised at the change in many a dreary day.

TUESDAY—FEBRUARY 29.

TODAY, I'd like to share these thoughts with you:

"Each day is a page of life — turn it with care."

"Love grows in the warmth of friendship, and blooms in the light of unselfishness."

March

WEDNESDAY—MARCH 1.

ISN'T it lovely to have Spring just round the corner, and isn't it marvellous to see all the magnificent flowers? I can never make up my mind whether I like best the gorgeous red and yellow tulips, the stately, upright daffodils, or the shy little violets and snowdrops.

I suppose, like people, it takes all sorts of flowers to make a garden. We can't all be flamboyant tulips or proud daffodils. Modest little violets and primroses have a lovely scent of their own, so they play their part equally well even if in a rather different way. In life we are all worthwhile, whatever our gifts or abilities.

THURSDAY—MARCH 2.

MANY of us have read with great pleasure those famous 18th-century classics "The Life Of Samuel Johnson" and "Journal Of A Tour To The Hebrides" by the Scottish writer and lawyer James Boswell. Friends and friendship were important to Boswell, and he had this to say about friendship:

"Friendship, the wine of life, should, like a well-stocked cellar, be continually renewed."

Wise words indeed!

FRIDAY—MARCH 3.

I LIKE the Chinese proverb which says: "Do not forget little kindnesses, and do not remember small faults."

Yes, do not forget small kindnesses received, and do not forget to do them in return, for little kindnesses warm the heart of those who receive them. And please do remember, too, what we may regard as small faults are much less worthy of our consideration.

SATURDAY—MARCH 4.

A PRAYER FOR SPRING

DEAR Lord of Creation,
As the earth awakes around me,
And all creatures rejoice with the Spring,
Let me, too, rejoice.
Let my heart be filled with thanksgiving,
Let me count my many blessings.
Go forward with me through the year.
Help me to travel cheerfully and hopefully,
Knowing You are near
And will always be my Friend.

Iris Hesselden.

SUNDAY—MARCH 5.

AND the servant of the Lord must not strive; but be gentle unto all men, apt to teach, patient.

Timothy II 2:24

MONDAY—MARCH 6.

ONE Spring morning I looked around the kitchen and noticed that the Lady of the House badly needed a new wooden spoon.

On receiving the new one, however, at first she told me that she couldn't use it as hers had become a real friend over the years. Later she told me that she realised she must always have been reluctant to change things in life.

"So I've decided that I will use my new spoon, Francis," she said, "and I'll adopt this new season for changing old for new, and bad for good. By doing that, I hope to become a more adaptable person. Now, do you think we could get to grips with computers next?"

TUESDAY—MARCH 7.

LEONARD CHESHIRE (1917-1992) was one of the outstanding men of his generation. As a young man he was a leading pilot in the Royal Air Force, and later in life was responsible for establishing worldwide many residential homes for disabled people. These words from him are well worth repeating:

"In my opinion, the great mission of those who suffer and are in want is to draw out the inherent goodwill that is in all of us, and so to make us forget ourselves and draw closer to one another in our common journey through life."

The Leonard Cheshire Foundation continues in strength on the same lines into the millennium — a fine memorial to a great man.

THE FRIENDSHIP BOOK

WE are all used to seeing so many slogans nowadays as a means of catching our attention, and here is a set with a difference from a church magazine in Billingham:

Bank on God for a higher rate of interest.

It's impossible for you to lose your footing on your knees.

Danger! Live Church!

Fight truth decay — brush up your Bible every day.

Come to church in March and avoid the Christmas rush.

PEACE is walking down a lane,
Dry earth refreshed by gentle rain;
It's glimpsing glowing stars at night,
And found in silent seabirds' flight.

It's found when Springtime gardens fill
With blossom and bright daffodil.
It's everywhere if you just look,
In music, art and well-loved book.

Open your eyes and you will find,
Beauty of sight and heart and mind,
For trees and moors and hills and dales,
Are where God's harmony prevails.
Chrissy Greenslade.

FRIDAY—MARCH 10.

DR David Munroe Cory was minister of a Presbyterian church in Brooklyn, New York, in the 1920s. When he found there was a colony of Mohawk Indians in the district he encouraged them to come along to his services. He learned their dialect and later translated hymns into it.

They called his church "O-non-sa-to-ken-ti-wa-ros-hors" which means "the church that makes friends".

Not a bad name for any church.

SATURDAY—MARCH 11.

ONE bright March day I donned my warm sweater and garden boots, then went out to inspect our vegetable patch. It was an uninspiring sight for it had been neglected during the cold Winter months. However, an hour or two's work with fork and barrow did wonders and soon it looked tidy again, ready for the Spring planting.

I find that gardening often has a lesson to teach us. Like most areas of life it is never too late to make a fresh start, and while the first move is often the hardest, everything we do after that nearly always brings improvement.

SUNDAY—MARCH 12.

AND now come I to thee; and these things I speak in the world, that they might have my joy fulfilled in themselves.

John 17:13

MONDAY—MARCH 13.

IN his book "To Be A Pilgrim" Cardinal Basil Hume wrote:

"I once met a high-powered businessman who told me that he had trained himself always to act towards other people on the assumption that he liked them. If he had a difficult person to deal with, or if he had dealings with one he disliked, he would ask himself, 'What would I do if I really liked that person?' He then did it."

Good advice for all of us to follow.

TUESDAY—MARCH 14.

THE Redwings Sanctuary in Norfolk was founded in 1984 by Wendy Valentine to give a home to horses, ponies and donkeys which have fallen on hard times. All are given a home until the end of their natural days, and they are looked after by skilled carers and a capable team of enthusiastic volunteers.

Most people have a soft spot for these animals, perhaps recalling childhood memories of the seaside. I like to think about donkeys, particularly on Palm Sunday, recalling that Jesus chose a donkey when he rode into Jerusalem as a sign that he came as Prince of Peace.

Here is a prayer written by a child from India: "O God, who created and loves all animals, help those that must work so hard, the oxen that have to pull heavy burdens, and donkeys that pull heavy loads. Care for hungry animals and make people kind to them."

WEDNESDAY—MARCH 15.

ONE of the most popular people the Lady of the House and I know is our friend Rose. You see, she possesses a very special talent — she is a wonderful listener.

I once complimented her on this attribute, and she looked surprised. "Oh, but I've never found it difficult to listen to others, Francis," she said. "Now, your comment just goes to show that old proverbs are not always right."

I looked perplexed and she laughed. "You've just proved that it's quite wrong to say that listeners never hear any good of themselves!"

THURSDAY—MARCH 16.

DURING the last few years, church members in the New Forest area have been sending out containers of clothing and useful items to one of the African countries with which they are linked. The project has been based on the Bible story of Tabitha in the Acts of the Apostles, who showed her love for God by making clothes for her neighbours.

During Lent one year, the 16 parishes worked together to fill more than 700 boxes and raised over £5,000 to pay for transport. Eight weeks later the consignment was in Africa.

The project was named "Containers Of Hope" for that is what it symbolised to those far away, not just for the material contents, valuable as they were, but for the fact that people they may never know have been concerned for their welfare.

FRIDAY—MARCH 17.

IN the 19th century Queen Victoria once wrote in her diary about the sermon she had heard in Crathie Church, near Balmoral.

"The minister explained," she wrote, "in the most beautiful and simple manner, what real religion is; how it ought to pervade every action of our lives; not a thing only for Sundays, or for our closet; not a thing to drive us from the world . . . but being and doing good, letting everything be done in a Christian spirit."

SATURDAY—MARCH 18.

"GRANDMA," gasped four-year-old Paul one day as he rushed in. "Guess what we've seen!"

Grandma didn't quite know where to start, as his world was so full of many exciting things. However, she was soon informed, "We've seen a rainbow."

She agreed that this was a wonderful sight and said she was sorry to have missed it. As someone once said: "Lord, keep within me the heart of a child." And then we can see what an exciting place this world really is!

SUNDAY—MARCH 19.

AND he shewed me a pure river of water of life, clear as crystal, proceeding out of the throne of God and of the Lamb.

Revelation 22:1

COOL CASCADE

MONDAY—MARCH 20.

HERE are some lovely old toasts from past days for us to share:

"May the winds of adversity never blow open your door."

"When we are going up the hill of fortune, may we never meet a friend coming down."

"May the honest heart never feel distress."

TUESDAY—MARCH 21.

WHAT a wonderful thing is song . . . One Sunday morning in the Spring of 1945, in a lane near Llangollen, a local journalist, Harold Tudor, heard a milk-boy singing a Welsh hymn. Thrilled by the sound, Harold thought how people from all over the world would love to hear such singing.

Out of that came the idea of a festival of song to encourage international friendship. It wasn't easy to make a start — a great deal of money had to be raised, and a network of contacts made — but Harold's hard-working group of enthusiasts succeeded in putting on the very first festival in 1947.

It has grown ever since, and today the Llangollen Eisteddfod is one of the major musical events in the European calendar with singers, instrumentalists and dancers coming from over 30 countries. Every year, new friendships are made and deeper understanding is created, all thanks to that singing milk-boy!

WEDNESDAY—MARCH 22.

"LOOK back and smile at perils past." I find these words by Sir Walter Scott both cheering and comforting. They remind me that many things we worry about never happen, and if they do, somehow or other we are given the ability to cope with them successfully, so that when all is over and in the past, we can indeed smile.

THURSDAY—MARCH 23.

FEW people visit the Lancashire lakeland coast without exploring the lovely village of Cartmel. The 12th-century Priory Church is particularly impressive.

The first time I visited it was when I attended a Sunday service there many years ago. The preacher suddenly stopped during his sermon and asked the congregation, "Who would miss you if you died tonight?"

At the time it did not unduly worry me, I must admit. I knew plenty of near relatives and friends who would certainly miss me and, of course, the Lady of the House. But I've never forgotten the question and sometimes it is one I ask myself.

I'll never know the answer, and neither will anyone else who hears the question. All we can hope for is that we will be remembered as happy, friendly people, always willing to give a helping hand to others, and show these traits because they are part of our natural character — not merely in the hope of a heavenly halo.

FRIDAY—MARCH 24.

I'VE never liked the saying, "You can't teach an old dog new tricks". I much prefer, "You're never too old to learn!"

The French writer, Georges Duhamel, surely had the right idea. He said life should be "a perpetual discovery". Look at it that way and it's amazing what you'll find out!

SATURDAY—MARCH 25.

MY friend Arthur is always ready with a bit of advice or philosophical reflection. Arthur had a busy working life as a plumber and once, when I was chatting to him, he admitted that as he got older, he was finding it more difficult to get up early in the morning to face a day's work.

Now Arthur is sixty-five years old and has been able to lay aside his box of tools. So when we last met I congratulated him on his retirement, and reminded him of his previous remarks.

"Well, Arthur, at least you don't have to get up at the crack of dawn to go to work, and you can have a 'lie in' in the morning," I said.

"Not likely," came the quick reply. "If you can get up early to go to work, you can get up early to play. I'm making the most of my retirement!"

SUNDAY—MARCH 26

AND he saith unto her, Daughter, thy faith hath made thee whole; go in peace, and be whole of thy plague.

Mark 5:34

MONDAY—MARCH 27.

A VISITOR once found the writer George Bernard Shaw wielding an axe as he chopped firewood. "That's hard work, Mr Shaw," he said.

GBS lowered the axe, his eyes twinkling. "That's what I like about it. Firewood should warm you three times. First, when you carry it home, then, when you chop it up, and lastly, when you burn it!"

Shaw always had his own way of looking at things, and he was often right!

TUESDAY—MARCH 28.

DR STANLEY JONES was once speaking to a Hindu audience during his missionary service in India. Some way through his talk, one of the listeners stood up and quite deliberately went out, returning soon afterwards, listening more intently than before.

After the meeting was over, the missionary asked why the lady had gone out when she did. Was she not interested?

"Oh, yes," came the reply, "I was so interested in what you were saying that I went out to ask your carriage driver whether you really meant what you said, and whether you lived this Christian way at home. When he said you did, I came back to listen again."

While it is much easier to preach than to practise, if the Gospel we proclaim makes no difference to our way of life, then we are wasting out time.

KEELS AND CREELS

WEDNESDAY—MARCH 29.

TOM, a friend of mine who is a great golf enthusiast, recently shot his first-ever hole-in-one during a competition at his golf club.

Tom proudly related this achievement to me and revealed that it is the custom to celebrate the event by inviting all your playing partners to a slap-up meal in the clubhouse, which he did. Knowing that Tom is not well off, I was concerned that this hole-in-one would have cost him a tidy sum which he could ill-afford.

"Never fear, Francis!" he said. "I'm insured. My policy covers me for up to £100 to cover celebrations for a hole-in-one!"

We normally insure ourselves against bad things happening, so I found it amusing to know that you can also insure yourself against something nice happening to you!

THURSDAY—MARCH 30.

COURTESY is like the air in tyres – it doesn't cost anything, but it makes travel a lot more comfortable.

FRIDAY—MARCH 31.

ANNE and Jim couldn't stand one another the first time they met. Now they're happily married! It's surprising how often this happens — we have to be careful not to judge folk too quickly.

As the writer Frank Swinnerton once commented: "Nine out of every ten people improve on acquaintance."

April

MY old friend, Ian, was in a philosophical mood one day when I found him surveying his garden with pride. There were many green shoots, fresh and new, to be seen in the gentle Spring sunshine.

"You know, Francis," he mused, "I've been thinking that love is like one of these tender plants."

"Why, Ian," I laughed, "you're an old romantic under that crusty exterior!"

He continued, "Love can't be forced. It will die in the cold, or from lack of attention. If it is warm and cared for, it will blossom beautifully. Unlike my plants, Francis, it grows stronger with time and will live for ever."

Later, I considered Ian's words. Love does need gentleness and kindness, and we should nourish our own tender plants with care. I'm sure that he is right — true love really does live for ever.

THE LORD looked down from heaven upon the children of men, to see if there were any that did understand, and seek God.

Psalms 14:2

MONDAY—APRIL 3.

DO you enjoy watching television programmes about stately homes and valuable antiques? The Lady of the House and I watch them from time to time and later, we often look around at our own possessions.

The vase on the table is not fine bone china and the chair in the corner is not an 18th-century one, but does it really matter? From my rather worn but very comfortable armchair by the window, I can see the garden, hear the birds and smell something delicious cooking in our kitchen! Add to this the blessing of good health and we surely have all the wealth we need.

I hope that you, too, are fortunate enough to feel the same — and long may it continue!

TUESDAY—APRIL 4.

THERE are sunny days within us
And Springtime thoughts to hold,
The gift of Summer memories
To warm the Winter's cold.
There are cheerful times within us
To cherish and to store,
The laughter and the happiness
Are there for evermore.
There's a quiet place within us,
A peace we can recall,
A treasure house of hope and joy
Lies deep within us all.

Iris Hesselden.

THE FRIENDSHIP BOOK

WEDNESDAY—APRIL 5.

DESPITE the seriousness of their calling, many ministers have an excellent sense of humour. I liked an item in a church newsletter from Yorkshire which listed a number of hymns to suit various professions. Here are some I recall:

Building Contractors — "The Church's One Foundation."

Census Takers — "All People That On Earth Do Dwell."

Dentists — "Crown Him With Many Crowns."

Golfers — "There Is A Green Hill Far Away."

THURSDAY—APRIL 6.

GEORGE BUSH, when President of the United States, was once busy entertaining members of the press corps and their families, when he found the young daughter of a television director crying bitterly beside the swimming pool.

She told him a "tragedy" had happened; she had lost a tooth — somewhere in the pool. As a parent Bush realised there was nothing to put under the pillow for the "Tooth Fairy". At once a Presidential Card was produced.

He put a big cross on the card with a sketched map and wrote: "Dear Tooth Fairy, Katie's tooth came out where the X is — it really did, I promise. George Bush." Katie had a certificate to put under her pillow, and not only was a little girl made happy but she had a lovely memory of a great man.

FRIDAY—APRIL 7.

DIANA, Princess of Wales, was famous for her visits to the sick, the homeless and deprived, visits often made in secret and at dead of night. She once explained her actions in these poignant words: "Someone's got to go out there and love people, and show it."

No wonder she is still mourned in the hearts of the poor and the rejected who knew in her a true friend.

SATURDAY—APRIL 8.

HOW do I know when Spring has arrived? Well, the Lady of the House usually tells me that a pair of blue tits has taken up residence in the nesting box in our garden.

For many of us, the first indication that Spring is on its way is when we see the first snowdrops appearing. For others it may be an awareness of lengthening days, catkins and pussy-willows on the trees, primroses in the hedgerow and lambs gambolling in the meadow — or even the first time we are able to mow the lawn.

Yet, whatever our own particular harbinger of Spring happens to be, we can all take heart in the words of Margaret Sangster: "Never yet was a Springtime when the buds forgot to blow."

SUNDAY—APRIL 9.

FOR Christ is the end of the law for righteousness to every one that believeth.

Romans 10:4

MONDAY—APRIL 10.

I'M sure I've told you before about our friend Mary's little notebook, in which she jots down all the thoughts and reflections that take her fancy. When the Lady of the House and I were once visiting her, Mary reached for her notebook and read out this quotation, one from the pen of the American writer Ralph Waldo Emerson:

"People seem not to see that their opinion of the world is also a confession of character."

Spare a few minutes to reflect on Emerson's words. I did, and found they gave me much food for thought.

TUESDAY—APRIL 11.

I GAVE my friend a pack of seeds
To cheer her through the Spring,
She sowed them in a tray of earth
They grew like anything.
So many seedlings that, in fact,
She passed some on next door.
Her neighbours put them in the ground —
You should have seen them soar.
The flowers bloomed so bright and fair,
A dazzling sight to see,
So plentiful that, can you guess?
Yes, some were passed to me.
It's nice to think that just like seeds,
Kind thoughts can grow and grow —
So sprinkle them with generous heart
You may reap what you sow!

Margaret Ingall.

BRIGHTON BELLE

WEDNESDAY—APRIL 12.

HAVE you ever noticed how grandmothers come in all shapes and sizes, especially nowadays when many are so remarkably young looking? When I think back to my own grandmothers and also my great-aunts they appeared to be rather elderly, and sometimes even a little aloof.

But the one thing all these ladies had in common — and still have, I'm pleased to say — is a great capacity for love. As the Lady of the House once remarked, they are rather like those delicious melt-in-the-mouth chocolate-coated marshmallows which we've all enjoyed — beautifully soft on the inside!

God bless all grandmothers and great-aunts, whatever their size and shape, and wherever they may be!

THURSDAY—APRIL 13.
UPS AND DOWNS

PLUSSES and minuses,
Roundabouts and swings,
Life's full of ups and downs —
It's just the way of things.

We cannot see the future,
We move on — come what may.
But if we reach rock bottom
"Up" is the only way!
             Dorothy M. Loughran.

THE FRIENDSHIP BOOK

FRIDAY—APRIL 14.

I WAS surprised when a friend said that the best thing to remember was how to forget. When I questioned John about this he said, "I read somewhere long ago that one path to happiness was to forget — to forget the faults of others, the lost opportunities and all the things in the past which we sometimes brood over.

"Some memories are golden and they shine more brightly when we remember to forget the ones that can take the gloss off our lives. It's not easy — but surely worth working at."

SATURDAY—APRIL 15.

*I*T'S *good to get away from noise,*
  From chaos and from din,
To seek in solitude and peace
  The beauty that's within.
To go into a quiet wood
  And breathe its loveliness,
To contemplate in silence
  Those things which calm and bless.

The mysteries of the universe,
  The wisdom of the sage,
Take some old and lovely thought
  From a bygone age,
And meditate upon the good,
  The honest and the true,
This calms the mind and you will find
  A blessing comes to you.
                    Kathleen Gillum.

SUNDAY—APRIL 16.

AND Thou, Lord, in the beginning hast laid the foundation of the earth; and the heavens are the works of thine hands.

Hebrews 1:10

MONDAY—APRIL 17.

THE famous Methodist preacher Lord Soper was well known for his quick wit. Once, when he was addressing a gathering at Speaker's Corner in Hyde Park, a heckler kept shouting, "What about flying saucers?"

"I'm sorry," said Lord Soper at last, "I cannot deal with your domestic problems here!"

TUESDAY—APRIL 18.

I'VE always wished that I could sing more melodiously but it doesn't stop me from singing the odd snatch of song in the privacy of my own home now and then.

As a guest at a young friend's wedding we were all asked to stand and sing "All Things Bright And Beautiful" and there was no holding me back. Here was a hymn I'd known since schooldays and I was determined to sing heart and soul. I needn't have worried about any imperfections, for the sound of my voice was lost among so many others around me.

You know, it's easy to forget just how many things there are in this world which are so Bright And Beautiful. It was a lovely reminder.

WEDNESDAY—APRIL 19.

MY thought for today comes from the writing of one of my favourite writers, Robert Louis Stevenson. In his "Memories And Portraits" he writes: "In every part and corner of our life to lose oneself is to be a gainer, to forget oneself is to be happy."

THURSDAY—APRIL 20.

THESE words of hope were seen scrawled on a wall in Capetown, South Africa:

"The road to the future is always under construction."

FRIDAY—APRIL 21.

ONE of the plants associated with the Christian calendar is the yellow flower which is known as Calvary Clover. Traditionally sown on Good Friday, it produces a prickly green seed pod which can have up to eleven seeds representing the eleven faithful disciples — but never twelve. When the seed pod is opened, it reveals a miniature crown of thorns and a scourge.

Calvary Clover grows in the Mediterranean countries and southern England. Each leaf has a blood-red mark, and legend tells us that it grew at the foot of the Cross and the leaves were spotted with the blood of Christ.

Since that day, it is said, the leaf has borne a red spot as a constant reminder to us of what happened on that first Good Friday.

SATURDAY—APRIL 22.

DO you like Easter eggs? The Lady of the House and I certainly do. Eggs are a symbol of continuing life, and the early Christians saw them as emblems of Christ rising from the tomb.

Some people boil their Easter morning egg with something such as cochineal to colour the shell. In Poland it is said that Mary painted eggs to amuse the baby Jesus and Polish mothers still do this.

The legend I like best, though, is about Simon of Cyrene. It is said that he was an egg seller and when he took the cross of Christ on his own shoulder on the road to Calvary, he left his basket on the roadside. When he returned, his eggs had been beautifully decorated.

When people denied themselves eggs and butter during Lent, a gift of fresh eggs at Easter would have been a treat. Nowadays when Lent is not so strictly observed, the usual custom is to give chocolate eggs to those we love.

I'll enjoy mine and, at the same time, I'll remember the true meaning of the custom.

SUNDAY—APRIL 23.

AND Jesus said unto him, Verily I say unto thee, To day shalt thou be with me in paradise.

Luke 23:43

MONDAY—APRIL 24.

GO cheerfully along life's road — who knows what we may find around the corner?

TUESDAY—APRIL 25.

AS I've mentioned before, Dr William Barclay has helped many people through his writings. Here is one of his prayers for the end of the day:

O God, my Father, as I lay me down to sleep,
Relax the tension of my body;
Calm the restlessness of my mind;
Still the thoughts which worry and perplex.

Let your Spirit speak to my mind and my heart while I am asleep, so that when I waken in the morning, I may find that I have received in the night-time —

Light for my way;
Strength for my tasks;
Peace for my worries;
Forgiveness for my sins.

WEDNESDAY—APRIL 26.

DO you ever wonder what sort of people our famous poets, musicians and novelists really were? It's said of John Keats that his face was always so radiant with brightness that it bore the expression of one who has just looked on some glorious sight.

Isn't that a wonderful way to be remembered?

THURSDAY—APRIL 27.

IT is sad that it has often become necessary to lock the doors of our churches. But the notice I caught sight of above just such a locked door was decidedly thought-provoking:

"I'm Out There."

FRIDAY—APRIL 28.

OUR dining-room clock once stopped so I put in a new battery, but it still wouldn't work. When our friend Peter, an engineer, called I told him about the clock.

He spent a few minutes making some adjustments, then gave it back to me. It was ticking away merrily.

"What was wrong?" I asked.

"Nothing, really," replied Peter. "It was just that you hadn't removed the price ticket from the battery so it wasn't making proper contact."

How often do we fail to make proper contact with our friends and neighbours to help them along life's way? By reaching out a helping hand, it can make all the difference.

SATURDAY—APRIL 29.

THE Lady of the House was clearing a vase of the very last of the Spring daffodils. "It's sad to see them go," I said.

"Not at all," she smiled. "Remember, the bulbs are still out there in the garden — they'll give us another vaseful or two next year. I'm looking forward to them already!"

And now I think about it, so am I!

SUNDAY—APRIL 30.

AND daily in the temple, and in every house, they ceased not to teach and preach Jesus Christ.

Acts 5:42

May

MONDAY—MAY 1.

I WAS fascinated watching the house martins building their nests under the eaves of some old farm buildings. These small Summer visitors arrive in May and are easy to distinguish as they fly backwards and forwards, busily making nests. They often return to places where they have nested in previous years, creating large colonies.

The first stage is laying a foundation of mud against the wall and when this is secure the nest is built on to it, patiently and gradually with beakfuls of mud and grass. Finally, it gets a thick layer of feathers to make a comfortable home for the new chicks. Should the nest become dislodged, the process starts all over again.

As far as good foundations, industry and patience are concerned, I think these birds have quite a lot to teach us.

TUESDAY—MAY 2.

ABRAHAM LINCOLN, President of the United States during the Civil War, declared:

"Most folk are about as happy as they make up their minds to be."

Aren't those words thought provoking? Let's think about them today.

EYES TO THE HILLS

WEDNESDAY—MAY 3.

I HEARD of a lovely idea from Scotland for celebrating the millennium. A young Ayrshire man, Craig Jamieson, set up a nursery which specialised in plants mentioned in the Bible. Myrrh, myrtle, tamarisk and pomegranate — Craig offered these and many others to customers who wanted the scents of the Holy Land in their own gardens.

What better way, this year, to be reminded of the world's greatest story?

THURSDAY—MAY 4.

"IF I only had a heart," said the Tin Man in the story "The Wizard of Oz". He wanted a heart so that he could be loving and caring.

Judith, a friend, has just told me a story that made me think of the Tin Man. She arrived at work one morning to find that her colleague was early and had started work. Everything, it seemed, had gone wrong so she was in a bad mood — nervous and angry with herself.

"The first thing I did to calm her down," said Judith, "was to take her for a coffee just to show her that she had a friend. We talked of other things until her mood improved."

I know very well that Judith always seems to have a kind heart, and uses it to care for, and feel for, those around her. The Tin Man so wanted to be like this.

Someone once said, "It is only with the heart that one can see rightly".

FRIDAY—MAY 5.

A NEW waiter turned up at a popular and busy restaurant. A regular customer, inquisitive by nature, questioned him about his workplace experience.

"I've been all over France," he replied, "gaining experience in as many restaurants and cafes as possible."

"Why didn't you stay in England and get the same experience at less expense? A rolling stone gathers no moss, you know."

"That may be true," came the quick retort, "but on the other hand if it gathers no moss it gets highly polished on the way."

There is often more than one way of looking at things and it's surely worth our while to think about them from many angles.

SATURDAY—MAY 6.

D R LESLIE WEATHERHEAD remarked on one occasion, "I don't believe it matters to God or the world whether a man is a butcher or a bishop. It does matter whether he is a good bishop or a good butcher."

It isn't the job, but the spirit in which the work is done which determines whether work is sacred or secular.

SUNDAY—MAY 7.

A S long as I am in the world, I am the light of the world.

John 9:5

MONDAY—MAY 8.

I WAS planting out my sweet peas one afternoon, when I remembered these lines by the poet John Keats from "I Stood Tiptoe Upon A Little Hill", and I wondered if you knew them:

Here are sweet peas, on tiptoe for a flight;
With wings of gentle flush o'er delicate white
And taper fingers catching at all things,
To bind them all about with tiny rings.

Isn't that a perfect description of how sweet peas grow? It's a lovely reminder of all the scents and colours of a Summer garden. It is, too, poetry written from the heart, for Keats said he found nothing more moving than the opening of flowers.

He would have agreed with Henry Ward Beecher, who remarked: — "Flowers are the sweetest things God ever made and forgot to put a soul in."

TUESDAY—MAY 9.

GROWING OLD

"WILL it happen?" he asks,
"Like a flash in the pan,
Young one day,
The next an old man."
"Definitely not,"
I say, in the know,
"It comes so slowly,
You don't see it grow."
                    Phyllis Ellison.

WEDNESDAY—MAY 10.

THE Lady of the House and I have a friend who declares: "I never look back, but always forward."

Now, looking forward is a splendid thing to do but when the going gets rough happy memories are a treasure to cheer us on our way. As Lord Elton once said: "The light we remember from yesterday was intended to illumine today and tomorrow."

THURSDAY—MAY 11.

IT is many years since Cicely Mary Barker's first book, the delightful "Flower Fairies Of The Spring" was published in 1923.

She was born in Croydon in 1895, and because she was a delicate child was educated at home. She was happiest when she had a sketch book in her hand, and taught herself to draw and paint, developing her individual style. Her first venture into the field of commercial art was at the tender age of 15 when she had a set of postcards published.

It was, however, her little volumes of "Flower Fairies" for each season, the wayside and the garden which brought her international acclaim. Each page contained a short poem written by herself — "Song Of The Willow Catkin" or "Song Of The Red Clover", perhaps, with a facing watercolour illustration of the flower fairy.

These classics of children's literature have been reissued, to enchant yet another generation.

SUNSET SYMPHONY

FRIDAY—MAY 12.

THE Lady of the House and I took a trip to Warwickshire to visit Shakespeare country. It's an area famous for its attractive thatched cottages and lovely villages. We were interested to learn that the old-time thatchers each had their own pattern which they wove into the ridge of the roof so that their work could easily be identified. An early form of trademark perhaps!

Nowadays, we recognise lots of things by their trademark — for example, cars, banks or clothing. It's nice to know that we each have our own particular trademark, too; the way we smile, our readiness to help, our patience in difficult situations. That is the way that those around us think about us and remember us.

SATURDAY—MAY 13.

I JUST thought I'd pass on to you, what our friend Alec said.

"You know, Francis, I always say 'au revoir' to you when you leave, but from today I am going to use a Turkish farewell — 'Go smiling'."

It sounds good to me.

SUNDAY—MAY 14.

BLESSED be the Lord, that hath given rest unto his people Israel, according to all that he promised: there hath not failed one word of all his good promise, which he promised by the hand of Moses his servant.

Kings I 8:56

THE FRIENDSHIP BOOK

HERE are a couple of thoughts to consider today:

Life is precious, handle prayerfully.

Life is full of small surprises and delightful moments. Treasure each and every one.

CHRISTIAN Aid Week is an opportunity for us to help bring clean water, food, healthcare and education to some of the poorest communities. It brings help to children such as 12-year-old Moti who lives in India. He walks up to eight miles each day carrying his shoe-shine brush, polish and mending thread, looking for customers. He earns very little but without this, his family would be even hungrier.

Let us keep in mind this special prayer:

Oh God, you give us freedom to live
*   according to our own desires,*
But we know your desire is
*   to have us follow you.*
Help us to come alongside those
*   whose freedom to live is limited*
By poverty, injustice and oppression.
Use our efforts to support their struggle
*   for a better life*
Which you want for all people.

Christian Aid believes in making long-term commitments to people in the Third World so that they can build a better future.

WEDNESDAY—MAY 17.

IT is so easy to misjudge people. Some assess others by the clothes they wear, or maybe by their accents. I read this story about T. E. Lawrence — Lawrence of Arabia. He lived in Dorset and was a great friend of the author Thomas Hardy and his wife.

Soon after Lawrence gave up his rank in the army and became an aircraftsman in the RAF, he went in uniform for his usual cup of tea and a chat with the Hardys. He found the mayoress of Dorchester present. Mrs Hardy, thinking that they knew each other, did not introduce them.

When the lady saw him she was disgusted, and told Mrs Hardy in French that she had never been asked to take tea before with an ordinary aircraftsman.

There was a long deep silence, until Lawrence said courteously, "I beg your pardon, madam, but can I be of any use as your interpreter? Mrs Hardy knows no French."

It is unwise to make quick judgments of others.

THURSDAY—MAY 18.

A MEMBER of the Samaritans was once asked about the greatest mistake she could make when answering a call. She replied, "Saying I understand before I have listened to the problem, finishing the person's sentences for him or her and, worst of all, thinking I know all the answers."

Good advice for us all, don't you think?

FRIDAY—MAY 19.

I WENT to see Bert who had had to leave his home and move into sheltered housing several miles away. I thought he would be lonely, but not a bit of it.

"Look," he grinned, "I've brought all my best friends with me." He pointed to his chair, his books and an old clock. "They all keep me company, just like they always did!"

SATURDAY—MAY 20.

THE Lady of the House and I called to see a friend one day and found Catherine busy in the kitchen. Cooling on a tray were cakes and buns. We apologised for interrupting and asked if she was having a party.

"Oh, no," she answered with a laugh, "only the family for tea, but it's almost like a party each time they appear."

We thought how lovely this was and what a warm welcome her family must receive when they come to visit. We can't all bake beautiful cakes, it's true, but if our welcome to family and friends is warm and sincere, then our visitors will feel very special. In fact, it could be "almost a party" every day.

SUNDAY—MAY 21.

AND ye shall know that I am in the midst of Israel, and that I am the Lord your God, and none else: and my people shall never be ashamed.

Joel 2:27

MONDAY—MAY 22.

ONE Monday, two tourists from Liverpool, on holiday in Canada, visited a small restaurant for lunch, and found that their table mats had different thoughts for every day of the week. They were very encouraged by the Monday message:

To watch the sun set in the west without regretting;
To hail its advent in the east — the night forgetting;
To have enough to share — to know the joy of giving;
To thrill with all the sweets of life — is living.

Maybe it is not prize-winning poetry, but it contains some lovely thoughts, all the same.

TUESDAY—MAY 23.
A PRAYER

GOD bless you every moment
  And keep you in His care,
God send you gifts of hope and joy
  And happiness to share.
God walk with you each morning
  And send His guiding light,
And may His everlasting peace
  Give restful sleep at night.
God take your hand in trouble,
  In turmoil and in strife,
And may the comfort of His love
  Forever fill your life.

Iris Hesselden.

WEDNESDAY—MAY 24.

WHAT a lot of changes the older generation has seen! You would think we would be used to them all by now, but though we might not admit it, many of us are still a bit suspicious of the new and strange.

As a wise old bishop once remarked, "We are all in favour of change — so long as it doesn't make any difference!"

THURSDAY—MAY 25.

A FRIEND of ours, Sandra, married a widower with four young children. She dearly loved them, and at first felt quite hurt when they kept telling her, "Our mummy always did it like this," and, "Mummy always said . . ."

However, Sandra never let them know how she felt. She asked the children to call her by her Christian name, and always introduced them to her friends as her stepchildren.

Then, one day it happened.

One morning as she was working, the eldest of the children, Paul, sat her down, looked her straight in the eye and said, "We've been discussing this together and we don't like you introducing us as your stepchildren. You are our mother now. We will always love our first mummy, but we love you, too."

Sandra told us that she choked back tears as Paul gave her a big hug — it was wonderful that they loved her so much. Her own unstinted love, patience and faith had worked this little miracle.

FRIDAY—MAY 26.

LAST year I watched a woodland being felled. A few slim birches were left standing, but alas, without the protection of the other trees around them, they were blown down in the first gale.

None of us can stand completely alone. We all need the help and support of one another, just like the trees in a wood.

SATURDAY—MAY 27.

FOR a number of years, I kept in touch with a very quiet friend. We used to meet occasionally and he was always pleasant and cheerful. As we parted, he would say, "Well, Francis, we'll see what another week brings."

He was much older than I was and, sometimes, this remark would irritate me.

As the years passed in rapid succession, though, I began to understand what James had meant. Sometimes a week would end on a quiet note, then Sunday would produce something quite unexpected. Another week might be filled with stress and disappointment, then suddenly, out of the blue, something uplifting would occur.

It's a long time now since James and I met, but I'll always remember him with pleasure. Often, on Sundays, the Lady of the House and I will smile at each other and say: "See what another week brings."

I hope that there will always be something pleasant for every one of us each week, exactly as I know James would have wished.

SUNDAY—MAY 28.

THEN he took the five loaves and the two fishes, and looking up to heaven, he blessed them, and brake, and gave to the disciples to set before the multitude.

Luke 9:16

MONDAY—MAY 29.

UNTIL recently the 14th-century church dedicated to St Ethelburga, sandwiched between shops, was the smallest church in the city of London. It survived the ravages of the Great Fire of 1666, the Blitz during the Second World War and later attempts to replace it with modern office blocks.

Sadly, it no longer exists, for it was destroyed in a bomb attack in 1993, yet, like all good things, it lives on in the memory of those who loved it, as will these words which were inside the porch.

These are the ten things for which no-one has yet been sorry:-

For doing good to all,
For being patient towards everybody,
For hearing before judging,
For thinking before speaking,
For holding an angry tongue,
For being kind to the distressed,
For asking pardon for all wrongs,
For speaking evil of none,
For stopping the ears to a tale-bearer,
For disbelieving most of the ill reports.

TUESDAY—MAY 30.

ST IGNATIUS of Loyola was born in 1491 the noble son of noble Spanish parents, and so was automatically trained to be a soldier. By the time of the Battle of Pamplona he was an army officer, with the prospect of a successful career ahead.

But then, a cannonball shattered his right leg and, during a long, weary recovery he had time to reflect. He wanted to read, but all that was available was a life of our Lord and a collection of lives of the saints. After his convalescence, he was to change his calling completely — to a life devoted to God.

He founded the Society of Jesus, and later composed that well-known prayer: "Teach us, good Lord, to serve Thee as Thou deservest, to give and not to count the cost, to fight and not to heed the wounds, to toil and not to seek for rest, to labour and to ask for no reward, save that of knowing that we do Thy will, through Jesus Christ our Lord."

WEDNESDAY—MAY 31.

MAGAZINE editors, I'm told, go to a lot of trouble to find a good cover illustration. But surely it's what's inside that really matters?

It's the same with people. We all have at least one close friend who didn't particularly impress us on that first encounter.

Often it's the ones with the poorest and plainest of "covers" who turn out the best.

June

A PRAYER FOR SUMMER

*D*EAR *Father of All — The earth is*
filled with beauty,
Fill my heart with joy and wonder.
Let me sing with the birds,
And marvel at the plants and flowers.
If clouds should darken my horizon
Let me be aware of Your bounty,
Your endless gifts and blessings,
And Your never-failing love.

Iris Hesselden.

YOUNG Sally went shopping with her grandfather who had, on a previous occasion, bought a lemon-scented air freshener for his car. Sally had loved the scent. But on this occasion she missed it, and asked what had happened to the lovely lemon smell.

"I think the air freshener is finished," her grandfather replied.

"You mean it's past its smell-by date?" came the unforgettable response.

SATURDAY—JUNE 3.

I CALL it my quiet hour, that last hour before I retire to bed. It is a time of thought and a little reading. I once came across these lines, and thought you would appreciate them as I did. They are from an old nursery rhyme, whose author is unknown.

Hearts, like doors, will ope with ease
To very, very little keys,
And don't forget that two of these,
Are "I thank you" – and – "If you please".

SUNDAY—JUNE 4.

B LESSED be he that cometh in the name of the Lord.

Psalms 118:26

MONDAY—JUNE 5.

I F you have ever started off tomato plants or flower seedlings on a sunny window-sill, you will have noticed how they respond to light. They instinctively turn their heads towards the sun and, to keep the plants straight, you need to rotate the pots so that the sun reaches all parts of them.

Most of us, too, feel happier when the sun is shining and a walk on the sunny side of the road, a little seat in the park or time spent with a good friend can do wonders for the way we feel.

As a saying I know advises: "Keep your face always towards the sunshine and the shadows will fall behind you".

TUESDAY—JUNE 6.

THE 16th-century writer John Lyly provides us with our thought for today. Born in 1554, he wrote: "Friendship, though it is plighted by shaking the hand, yet it is shaken off by fraud of the heart."

I have written these words in my notebook, for it is surely a quotation to remember well, don't you agree?

WEDNESDAY—JUNE 7.

I WAS interested to read that ten profoundly deaf people in the diocese of Lichfield completed a two-year course in religious studies and had been awarded the Bishop's Certificate.

Both men and women, including two sets of husbands and wives, were among those completing the studies, and although the course was modified, it was essentially the same as that followed by hearing people. Michael Sabell, Senior Chaplain, said, "It is the first time that deaf people have been involved in the course. I'm delighted at the group's achievement although we obviously had to rely heavily on sign language."

Now, four of the group will go on to be licensed lay readers in different parishes and two more will become diocesan lay workers. It's a fine example of what can be achieved by people with a disability when they set out with courage and determination — and when there are people alongside them who are sensitive to their needs.

THE FRIENDSHIP BOOK

THURSDAY—JUNE 8.

FOR some reason I woke early one morning, a song buzzing around in my head. It was all rather vague, as I hadn't heard the words for many years. The words continued to haunt me — something about being "shown the morning".

Quietly, I got up and went to the window. Drawing back the curtains. I looked out at the dawn. It was breathtaking!

The sky was ablaze with glorious colours. From red to the palest pink; eggshell blue to mauve. The air was fresh and clean and everything felt new. How long I stayed there, gazing out, I don't know. Only the birds were stirring, beginning their first song of the day. Along the horizon, the trees were silhouetted against the sky as if etched by some unseen hand.

Gradually, the colours faded and, returning to bed, I wished those moments could have been captured and preserved for ever. As I drifted off to sleep, at peace with the world, I gave thanks that I had been shown that very special morning.

FRIDAY—JUNE 9.

THE Lady of the House and I like to pause and read the posters outside churches. Here are two thoughts from these "Wayside Pulpits":

"Three little words to light the day —
    God Loves You."
"Love can't be measured or stored every day,
    It only increases when given away."

SATURDAY—JUNE 10.

PRINTED in "Punch" in 1875, I think the message of this rhyme is just as appropriate today as it was then:

There was an old owl liv'd in an oak
The more he heard, the less he spoke;
The less he spoke, the more he heard
O, if men were all like that wise bird!

SUNDAY—JUNE 11.

BLESSED be the Lord God of Israel for ever and ever. And all the people said, Amen, and praised the Lord.

Chronicles I 16:36

MONDAY—JUNE 12.

WALKING along the beach near the water's edge, a friend, Duncan, noticed thousands of starfish washed up from the previous tide. There were many of them, only a few feet from the water, all stranded.

He bent down, picked one up, and gently threw it back into the sea. He reached down again, and did the same with another. And then another . . .

A man walking his dog along the beach saw what was happening, and asked: "Why are you doing that? Surely you can't make a difference to all these starfish — there are too many of them."

But, as he threw yet another back into the sea, the first man replied, "Maybe, but it's definitely made a difference to this one!"

OPEN HOUSE

TUESDAY—JUNE 13.

SOME time ago, the Lady of the House and I lived near a man called Alan. He was very artistic and enjoyed drawing, painting and calligraphy. His family once told us how all their birthday cards arrived beautifully hand-lettered.

While talking to Alan one day, we were surprised to learn that he had no appreciation of music and he regretted that he should be deprived of something which gives others so much pleasure. However, we came to the conclusion that, as he saw beauty in nature, perhaps he found a sort of music there, too — maybe the rustle of the wind in the trees, the pattering sound of rain on a window or the lively blackbird's early serenade.

The Lady of the House summed it up quite neatly. "You know, Francis," she said, "Alan has probably discovered the music of life."

Indeed. Perhaps he hears far more than the rest of us, and we may be the ones who should listen more carefully.

WEDNESDAY—JUNE 14.

WHEN leafing through a book of quotations, I found these sayings and I'd like to pass them on to you:

Contentment comes with the knowledge that all is well with those we love.

Never look back — except in forgiving;
Always look forward — life is for living!

THURSDAY—JUNE 15.

IT was one of those grey overcast mornings when Alfred came along the street towards me, whistling a merry tune.

"You're cheerful," I said, "despite the clouds!"

"Of course," he grinned. "The sun's still up there, you know. It's just that we can't see it. But we will!"

And by afternoon we did!

FRIDAY—JUNE 16.

SUNDAY school teachers sometimes have problems in explaining to young people that no matter how difficult life is, Jesus will never let them down.

I have been reading how Tom Rees, the evangelist, tackled the problem with some Cockney youngsters who could not be convinced of this. He asked one to hold on to him, whatever happened next.

The boy gripped his wrists, but soon found that the stronger man could break away. Then the evangelist suggested doing things the other way round, and he held the boy's wrists saying, "Now you try to get free." This proved impossible.

"Why did we come apart the first time?" asked Tom Rees.

"That's easy," the boy replied. "The first time I had hold of you, now you've got hold of me." The message went home.

Being a Christian is not holding on to Christ — but being held by Him.

SATURDAY—JUNE 17.

I AM glad that fathers now have their own special day when families show them their love and appreciation. This Father's Prayer was written more than 30 years ago, but I'm sure you'll agree that it is just as relevant today:

"O God, help me to be true to the great privilege and the great responsibility which you have given me; help me to be an example and a friend to my children and a real partner to my wife; don't let me take all that is done for me for granted, and help me to keep love alive within the home.

"Give me health and strength and work to do to earn a living for those who depend on me and whom I love so much; but help me to remember that love is always more important than money."

God bless all fathers on their special day!

SUNDAY—JUNE 18.

BLESSED are the pure in heart: for they shall see God.

Matthew 5: 8

MONDAY—JUNE 19.

THE 18th-century politician and writer, Edmund Burke, once said, "Nobody makes a greater mistake than he who did nothing because he could do only a little."

How right he was!

THE FRIENDSHIP BOOK

TUESDAY—JUNE 20.

A YOUNG minister had been invited to be guest preacher at a church. He went to see the verger and asked nervously, "What do you think I should preach about?"

"About ten minutes," replied the verger.

WEDNESDAY—JUNE 21.

RETURNING from the post office early one morning, I met sisters Jane and Emma.

"Where are you going in such a hurry?" I asked.

"To Mum's," replied Jane. "With her birthday present," added Emma, grinning broadly. As they weren't carrying any parcels, I was puzzled, until the next day when the Lady of the House and I visited their mother, Kate, on her 70th birthday, with our own gift for her.

We found Kate relaxing at home, which was tidy and polished from top to bottom, and her larder full to bursting with food of all kinds.

"My daughters did this yesterday as my birthday present," she explained. "You see, I'd said that I just didn't want any more items that need dusting. So they hit upon this idea of giving my home a 'Spring clean' and stocking up my fridge and larder. Now, just see what they've written on my card . . .

"We promise to do this for you,
For Christmas, Easter, Birthday, and
dear Dad's birthday, too.

"Now that's what I call 'home help' at its very best," remarked the Lady of the House.

THURSDAY—JUNE 22.

THE pessimist is someone,
* Who is rather keen to bring*
A strange philosophy that sees
* The gloom in everything.*
The optimist is someone,
* Who can visualise a way*
To make the future bright, and keep
* The pessimist at bay.*

J. M. Robertson.

FRIDAY—JUNE 23.

WHEN little Daniel and his parents came to stay with us, we found that he was a very light sleeper and the squeaking of the upstairs doors woke him a few times the first evening.

"You had better try a drop or two of oil, Francis," said the Lady of the House the next morning.

Sure enough, that small drop did the trick. Daniel was able to sleep peacefully and the rest of us were able to relax.

Very often a "spot of oil" at the right time can not only help to put things right, but can also prevent them going wrong in the first place. I'm thinking about an encouraging smile, a word of praise when somebody has tried hard, a comforting hug when someone has failed, or holding our tongue when we are sorely tempted to speak a word of criticism — in fact, all the things that can do so much to keep our lives and relationships running smoothly.

SATURDAY—JUNE 24.

"THE secret of happiness is to forget oneself; it is rather like falling in love, I suppose, but that does not take so long."

Did you smile a little, when you read those words by Arthur Bryant? I did, just a little ruefully.

SUNDAY—JUNE 25.

OWE no man any thing, but to love one another: for he that loveth another hath fulfilled the law.

Romans 13:8

MONDAY—JUNE 26.

DO you ever read the details issued by estate agents? They usually consist of glowing descriptions and glossy colour photographs. We caught sight of some properties being described in our local paper one day, and they all looked wonderful.

The Lady of the House studied them for a little while and then announced: "Beautiful houses, Francis, but not necessarily comfortable homes."

Surprised, I asked what she meant.

"Well, think of these words," she said. " 'A house that does not have one piece of chipped china or worn mat in it, is soulless'. Now, can you imagine worn or chipped items in any of these houses?"

I had to admit that I couldn't, and I then looked round fondly at my own home. Who needs a mansion to be happy and comfortable?

THE FRIENDSHIP BOOK

I HAVE several friends who are not very tall and complain they find it difficult to reach items on the top shelves of supermarkets. Some console themselves by saying, "Good stuff goes in little room!", but lack of height can be a nuisance.

A story I once read had an interesting slant on the problem. A tiny lady in a supermarket asked a tall man if he would kindly pass her an item from the top shelf. She thanked him warmly as he did so and, looking up at his tall stature, added, "Do you need anything from down here?"

Very thoughtful!

YOUNG Joanne often struggles with her schoolwork, so usually she is not in the forefront when awards are being handed out. Consequently, her mother was extremely pleased when she came home from school and said she had been given a sticker to put on the class's achievement chart.

"Well done!" said her mother. "What did you do to win it?"

"I was kind to someone," Joanne replied.

Apparently, one of her classmates had been in tears in the playground. Joanne had gone across to comfort her and this response had been noticed by one of the staff.

I'm glad Joanne got that sticker. As for me, I would rather win a medal for kindness than for anything else at all. How about you?

THURSDAY—JUNE 29.

PERHAPS doing the washing-up is not most people's favourite job but there is another way of looking at it, as this rhyme points out:

Thank God for dirty dishes,
They have a tale to tell,
For by this pile that I have here,
It seems we're living well.
While others there are starving,
I've not the heart to fuss,
For by this pile it's evident
God's very good to us.

FRIDAY—JUNE 30.

THERE'S a story about an Indian man who was walking home at nightfall. As he made his way along the path, he was startled to see a snake lying across it. In his panic to get away, he tripped and fell, picked himself up and then ran shouting to his village.

His friends quickly fetched some lanterns and accompanied him back to where the snake had been seen. It was still there across the path, but by the light of the lanterns they could see quite clearly that what he had thought to be a snake was just a piece of old rope.

So often we make wrong assumptions about people and situations, causing ourselves much unnecessary anxiety. A little time for taking stock usually puts things into perspective, and what at first appears threatening often turns out to be as harmless as that old piece of rope.

July

SATURDAY—JULY 1.

ONE of our neighbours Lilian was looking very pensive one Monday evening.

"Did you have a nice weekend visiting your son?" I asked.

"Yes, I did," she replied, "and that's what I was thinking about. You see, in all the various stages of Kevin's life, I think I have guided him along the right paths — friends, school, career, and so on. Then this weekend I offered to mow the lawn at his new home. I was to be the first ever to cut it.

"I tried to make the lines straight, so that ever after, when Kevin mowed, he could follow the lines I'd made."

This set me thinking of the responsibilities a parent has to their child by always guiding them along the straight and narrow road of life. As Lilian said: "I hope I didn't wander too much with the mower, and that the lines were a good guide, Francis."

SUNDAY—JULY 2.

AND hereby we do know that we know him, if we keep his commandments.

John I 2: 3

THE FRIENDSHIP BOOK

MONDAY—JULY 3.

THIS is how the Victorians described a friend using the language of flowers. All the qualities represented are valuable attributes of friendship, whatever age we live in.

Forget-me-not — True love;
Rose — Love;
Ivy — Fidelity;
Elm — Dignity;
Nightshade — Truth;
Dogwood — Durability.

TUESDAY—JULY 4.

IF you want to do a thing
Then do it right away.
Start it — don't procrastinate
Proceed with it today.
Just say the kindly words you feel
And do the timely deed,
Tomorrow may be too late
To meet somebody's need.

Make an effort of the will
To make a brand-new start.
Mend all quarrels — cast aside
The fears that haunt the heart.
Resolve to make life work for you
Don't question when or how,
Just put the wheels in motion —
The time to start is now.

Kathleen Gillum.

WEDNESDAY—JULY 5.

ONE day, Father Andrew Lawler was driving through a Kenyan game park when his vehicle broke down. He investigated the problem and, while he was busy, a young Masai tribesman offered to help. Father Lawler thought he would try a little evangelism.

"Do the Masai pray?" he asked.

"Oh, yes, we pray hard every day."

"And what do you pray for?"

"That God will bless us with many cows, many children and many wives," came the response.

"And has God blessed you?"

The young man replied, "Oh, yes. I have many cows, many children and many wives." And then he asked Father Lawler, "Do you have many cows?"

"No," replied the priest.

"Many children?"

"No, I have no children."

"But do you have many wives?"

"No," Father Lawler laughed. "I have no wives."

The young Kenyan looked perplexed, and then he said, "You know what your problem is, don't you? You should pray more often!"

THURSDAY—JULY 6.

"HAPPINESS is a plant which will grow in any soil that is watered in love and service, but withers in the hot sunshine of selfishness."

W. Riley.

FRIDAY—JULY 7.

L AUGHTER, they say, is the best medicine and I'm sure it's true. One of my favourite quotations is also the shortest: "He who laughs, lasts."

SATURDAY—JULY 8.

O UR friend Susan told us this story recently. "When my parents were married," she said, "and that was more than 80 years ago, a small boy, the son of a friend of theirs, was most upset when he saw everybody giving wedding presents, for he himself had nothing to give.

"Then with sudden inspiration he offered, very seriously, a pip from an apple he had been given. To humour him, Mother planted it in the garden where it grew into a magnificent tree."

Susan continued, "Our apple tree was to be a continual source of delight. In Spring it was covered with pink blossom which brought pleasure to us and our neighbours. In the Autumn we had so many luscious apples that Mother used to give them away. As a bonus Father made a swing for us on one of the branches."

What a lot of pleasure was given to so many from that apparently insignificant wedding gift. Most of the other presents would have been lost, broken or just worn out, but the apple tree gave decades of pleasure.

Even the smallest gift — perhaps just a kind word or a thoughtful deed — can bring so much happiness.

SUNDAY—JULY 9.

THE Lord is gracious, and full of compassion; slow to anger, and of great mercy.

Psalms 145:8

MONDAY—JULY 10.

I ONCE made the mistake of thinking someone was lonely simply because he was standing alone, leaning over a gate leading to a meadow beyond. I stopped to chat with this stranger, and found him to be a man at perfect peace with his surroundings, enjoying his own company.

I didn't stay long as he wasn't in need of conversation, but as I left I realised what a wonderful gift this man was blessed with. He had contentment within himself, and so knew little of loneliness or boredom. As most of us are alone at some time or another, wouldn't it be nice if we, too, could learn to enjoy our own company, and find peace and contentment there?

TUESDAY—JULY 11.

LOOKING through the pages of "The Book Of Royal Lists", I came across these sayings which I'm sure you'll enjoy sharing today:

"Your work is the rent you pay for the room you occupy on earth."

The Queen Mother.

"Look after the children and the country will look after itself."

King George VI.

THE FRIENDSHIP BOOK

<u>WEDNESDAY—JULY 12.</u>

TRAVELLER'S TALE

I'LL journey again down Memory Lane
   To remember so much from the past.
Faces and places, and positive traces
   Of memories destined to last.
The laughter, the tears, some regrets through
      the years
   In an album the mind can compile —
I'll journey again down Memory Lane
   It's a journey that's proving worthwhile.

                              J. M. Robertson.

<u>THURSDAY—JULY 13.</u>

"IT'S raining again!" I once observed loudly. We were on holiday in the Lake District at the time and felt so sorry for a party of schoolchildren we met returning from a day outdoors, their clothes dripping, their boots mud-caked. It seemed such a pity that their holiday should be spoiled by the weather, and I expressed sympathy.

"Thank you," said their teacher-in-charge. Then he grinned and continued, "Do they look as if they need sympathy?"

They were laughing, singing — in fact, the picture of happiness. "We've had so much fun," said one youngster. "We've paddled in streams, sploshed through mud, slid down pathways . . ."

It all depends on your viewpoint, doesn't it? The memory of these contented children made me change my attitude towards the weather, not only that morning, but on many rainy days thereafter.

FRIDAY—JULY 14.

I WAS sitting chatting to our old friend Mary one afternoon as she reminisced about her schooldays.

"I wasn't particularly clever," she recalled, "and I had great difficulty doing sums, but when Grandmother came to tea she never asked if I had been a good girl or got my sums right. She would say, 'Have you progressed?' — and how pleased I was when I could reply 'Yes'."

We may sometimes regret that we haven't the talents and abilities of some of those around us, but I'm sure the important thing is to know we have done the best with what we have.

SATURDAY—JULY 15.

IRENE'S grandfather was feeling low. He lives with her and her family in London far from the country town where he was brought up. She knew he wished he was back there, but that was impossible. Then she had a brainwave.

She bought a collection of old postcards of the town and presented them to him. Once again he could walk the old streets and see the familiar faces and old shops. "He's like a young man again," says Irene. "It's the best buy I ever made."

SUNDAY—JULY 16.

FOR the kingdom of God is not meat and drink; but righteousness, and peace, and joy in the Holy Ghost.

Romans 14:17

MONDAY—JULY 17.

A MORNING PRAYER

HERE comes another morning, Lord,
The dark of night has flown,
Remind me, as this day begins,
I never walk alone.
Be with me every single step
Through all I see and do,
And when my heart is heavy, Lord,
Then help me turn to You.
Be with me as the twilight comes
So silent round my door,
And help me to remember, Lord,
You'll stay with me, once more.

Amen.

TUESDAY—JULY 18.

I'M sure you must know how fond I am of collecting quotations! I love the way they can change our perceptions, cast new light on old truths or make us smile. Perhaps one of my favourite quotations, from the writer E.M. Forster, is also one of the shortest: "Only connect."

At first these words puzzled me, but the more I thought about them, the more sense they made. You see, if we can "only connect" with each other, deliberately using our imagination to build bridges rather than barriers, then how much easier it becomes to appreciate others, and to understand and tolerate their weaknesses.

And with any luck, they will be making the same effort and allowances for us!

WEDNESDAY—JULY 19.

I MET my old friend, Colin, returning from his regular morning walk with his dog, and he was chuckling happily.

"I've just had a letter," he said. "Look!" He handed me a sheet of drawing paper. On it was a child's drawing of a blue rabbit, and below it in childish script: "Thank you for finding me. Love and kisses from Bunny."

"I'll pin this up on the wall," he said. Then he told me how he had come to receive it.

Apparently, when walking his dog in the park one day, he'd found a toy on the path, and as it was beginning to rain he'd sat it on a seat in a park shelter. Happily, its rightful owner found it, and the result was this note left pinned to the wall.

You can imagine the joy of the sorrowing owner on finding Bunny. Then the joy was passed on to Colin in the thank-you note, then he in turn passed it on to me, and now I've passed it on to you . . . A happiness chain is being forged.

THURSDAY—JULY 20.

THE young Earl of Surrey, who was executed by Henry VIII, provides this thought for us to reflect on today:

The things that do attain
The happy life be these, I find,
The riches left, not saught with pain
The fruitful ground, the quiet mind.

FRIDAY—JULY 21.

IN these days of such advanced technology it is good to be reminded that old country skills have not died out. Take a craft like dry stone walling; experts can build a wall without a dab of mortar. It seems amazing that the stones can stand up like this.

Once at an agricultural show, an onlooker watched with great admiration as a craftsman demonstrated his skills with stone, then asked, "What makes these walls stand up?" A quick response followed: "The fellow who builds 'em!" That surely says it all.

Computers may be marvellous but there are some things they can never do.

SATURDAY—JULY 22.

I DON'T know who wrote these lines but they always give me fresh heart and I hope they will do the same for you:

When things go wrong, and they sometimes will,
When the road you're tramping seems all uphill,
When funds are low and debts are high,
And you want to smile, but you have to sigh,
When care is pressing you down a bit,
Rest, if you must, but don't you quit!

SUNDAY—JULY 23.

TRUST in the Lord with all thine heart; and lean not unto thine own understanding.

Proverbs 3:5

MONDAY—JULY 24.

DEREK has an interesting and unusual hobby. He collects semi-precious stones, or even promising-looking small pebbles from the sea-shore and polishes them. When the process is completed, they can be made into attractive jewellery.

What is fascinating is that in their original state the stones may be dark, dull looking and not very attractive. It is the friction which removes the flaws and reveals the full beauty beneath.

I believe that the same thing also applies to people. It is often the trials of life which bring out the true beauty of character — patience, love, thoughtfulness and serenity — qualities which may otherwise have remained hidden.

TUESDAY—JULY 25.

ALEX was a down-and-out in an Edinburgh hostel. One day he began to paint a mural on the lounge wall.

It was a bleak, grey landscape but, over time, as he grew better, the colours grew warmer and the scene brightened. Blue skies replaced the grey just as they were doing in his own life. Alex painted his way to recovery and a new beginning.

WEDNESDAY—JULY 26.

THE most wonderful discovery true friends can make about each other is that they can grow separately without growing apart.

THURSDAY—JULY 27.

I WAS searching through a dictionary of quotations when I stumbled across a verse that was new to me, "On Monsieur Coue":

This very remarkable man
Commends a most practical plan:
You can do what you want
If you don't think you can't,
So don't think you can't, think you can.

These words were written by Charles Inge, an English cleric who lived in the first half of this century. We might all take them to heart, surely.

FRIDAY—JULY 28.

ONE of our friends, Avril, is a very keen gardener, but I have often noticed that despite her skill in growing exotic plants, she is still quite happy to let the most humdrum of cottage garden plants thrive amongst them.

"When I first began gardening," she told me, "I was very ambitious. Anything as ordinary as forget-me-nots or marigolds I pulled out at once, to make quite sure they didn't spoil the elegance of my 'aristocrats.' It wasn't until some time later that I realised if only the rarer blooms were allowed, my garden would become more boring than when I started. Now I like to encourage all my flowers, however humble.

"After all, it takes all sorts to make a world, so I don't see why the same thing shouldn't apply to a garden!"

PERFECT PEACE

SATURDAY—JULY 29.

WHEN life seems to be going through a difficult patch, try to think about these wise words:

In the darkness of the night sky — see a star,
In the greyness of the mist — glimpse a glimmer of light,
On the bleak moorland — catch sight of a sheltering rock,
In the deep awe-filled silence — hear a song,
In the night of despair — the dawn will come,
And on that seemingly never-ending straight road — there will be a bend.

Be ready to see the hints, the signs of change, however small they may be. Wait and trust, the meaning will become clear. Keep hope in your heart.

SUNDAY—JULY 30.

JESUS said unto him, If thou canst believe, all things are possible to him that believeth.

Mark 9:23

MONDAY—JULY 31.

I'D like to share these wise sayings with you today:

Wherever we travel, there is a little corner of the heart called "Home".

The foolish man counts his riches, the wise man counts his blessings.

August

TODAY is 1st August, and in days gone by was celebrated as Lammas Day. The name comes from the Anglo-Saxon word "hlafmaesse" which means Loaf Mass Day, and was the day when women brought a loaf of bread baked from the new season's flour to church as an act of thanksgiving. The idea came from the Old Testament belief of offering the first fruit of the crops to God.

As we prepare for the full harvest thanksgiving services still to come, here is a grace for this season which you may like to use:—

Be with us at our table when we dine,
For all life's mercies, Lord, are gifts of thine.
Grant us thy blessings on our daily bread,
And over all our lives, thy radiance shed.

NOBODY wants to make an enemy. But sometimes it can happen. What should we do about it? Well, I think the best advice came from Cardinal Newman who said that we should "treat our enemy as if he were one day to be our friend".

That way, he probably will!

THURSDAY—AUGUST 3.

OUR friend Joe sometimes has a tendency to look on the gloomy side. We had been enjoying a particularly fine spell of weather that had brought everyone outdoors.

"What a lovely day, and such good growing weather, too!" someone remarked cheerfully.

"Maybe," said Joe, "but it won't last."

"Perhaps not," was the reply, "but I'm going to make sure I enjoy it while it's here."

Now there's the spirit!

FRIDAY—AUGUST 4.

IT doesn't seem so long ago
  I heard the other grandmas say,
"It's nice to see the children come,
  But nice to see them go away."
And as I listened to these words,
  I used to think, "What funny folk!"
I'm sure I'll never be like that —
  Or did they mean it as a joke?

But suddenly my turn has come,
  The kids arrive with clockwork mouse,
With squeaky dog, with chairs and clothes
  And in ten seconds — fill my house!
I'm older now and wiser, too,
  And so I've joined the ones who say,
"I love to see the children come."
  Then — shattered — wave them on their way.

                                    Iris Hesselden.

SATURDAY—AUGUST 5.

HERE are some thoughts on the company of books to share with you today:

"Books are the quietest and most constant of friends." Charles W. Eliot.

"A good book is the best of friends, the same today and for ever." Martin Tupper.

"Finishing a good book is like leaving a good friend." William Feather.

SUNDAY—AUGUST 6.

DRAW nigh to God, and he will draw nigh to you.

James 4:8

MONDAY—AUGUST 7.

I HAVE a friend, Margaret, who has what she calls a "daisy lawn", which presents her with a problem during the Summer. She simply can't quite bring herself to mow across them but she eases her conscience by picking as many as she can before mowing, then she arranges them in small vases on window-sills and ledges all around her home.

Such back-breaking work makes me wonder if she should perhaps put up a sign for passers-by saying:

"Pick Your Own Daisies — as many chains as you want."

I'm sure she'd have plenty of customers!

TUESDAY—AUGUST 8.

THIS verse was sent by a friend from her church magazine. It was printed as a thought to start off the year, but what a positive way it is to start every new day:

Be cheery, not dreary
Be happy, not sad.
Be carefree, despair free
Begin now — be glad.

WEDNESDAY—AUGUST 9.

WHAT makes a person successful? One who reaches a high-ranking position, and makes a fortune? Well, that might be the answer that springs to many people's minds.

Yet the most successful person I have ever met is Ted, a handyman and jobbing-gardener. He has a kindly word for everyone, and helping others has always been his way of life. He'd go out of his way time and time again to oblige when he saw the need was urgent, and often wouldn't take payment. He's too old to work now — but not too old to give passers-by a cheery wave from his window.

Such courtesy and consideration for others throughout the years is remembered, for it is now reflected in the care and help he is given — gladly — by friends and neighbours. Not that Ted was expecting this, it's just that he's been totally successful in encouraging kindness in others — and that's an achievement worth far more than a fortune and high rank.

THE FRIENDSHIP BOOK

THURSDAY—AUGUST 10.

I FOUND these thought-provoking lines in a Welsh parish magazine:

Blessed are those who can laugh at themselves,
They will have endless amusement.
Blessed are those who can tell a mountain
*   from a molehill,*
They will be spared a lot of trouble.
Blessed are those who are intelligent enough
*   not to take themselves seriously,*
They will be appreciated by those around them.

FRIDAY—AUGUST 11.

THIS story of animal behaviour caught my eye when reading by the fireside. A rider on horseback was making his way along a bridleway when he came upon a wounded pigeon on the path ahead. The horse came to a stop and stood trembling with fear, until the bird fluttered away.

What a strange thing, we might say, a horse afraid of a small bird, and an injured one at that. But this tale might remind us that animal behaviour is often not unlike our own. Think of those who draw back when confronted by people with severe disabilities. It may seem to be easier to avoid them than to try to understand and approach them. Animals and man have irrational fears.

Isn't it inspiring that we have the example of Jesus to follow — He was not afraid to touch lepers, the lame and the blind. He showed that love can soon conquer fear.

THE FRIENDSHIP BOOK

SATURDAY—AUGUST 12.

OUR friend Edna had to wait quite a time for her cataract operation and, as a result, some of her household jobs had to be put to one side. After her recovery one of the first things she planned to do was to deep clean her sitting-room carpet which she felt must be getting rather grubby.

"And do you know, Francis," she said, "once I could see properly, I had a good look at the carpet and I found that it didn't need cleaning after all."

Truly, blessings come in many guises!

SUNDAY—AUGUST 13.

FOR he is not a God of the dead, but of the living: for all live unto him.

Luke 20:38

MONDAY—AUGUST 14.

OCCASIONALLY I hear people grumbling that it is "too late" for them to change their ways, or to try something new. However, I came across this short poem listing some things for which it is never too late:

It's never too late to smile at a stranger,
It's never too late for encouraging words,
It's never too late to pause and to savour
The perfume of petals, the song of the birds.
It's never too late to say that you're sorry,
To offer your friendship, or bury your hate,
To send up a prayer, or to simply say "thank you",
It just takes a second — it's never too late!

TUESDAY—AUGUST 15.

WHY not take a little time today to think about these wise words?

Learn lessons from the past,
Look forward to the future,
Enjoy the present!

Don't let yesterday's disappointment cloud tomorrow's dream.

WEDNESDAY—AUGUST 16.

WE are constantly being told to keep an eye on our elderly neighbours, but how many of us do? Most of us tend to be rather preoccupied with our own affairs.

When Dorothy went into hospital, we heard that few folk had gone to visit her or had sent get-well cards. Her niece, who travelled several miles daily to the hospital, was concerned to see how downcast her aunt was.

However, a few days later a neighbour started to collect money to send Dorothy a lovely bouquet with a note saying how much we all missed her. Her niece later told us that, from the minute she received the flowers, she became brighter and there was a marked improvement because Dorothy realised that neighbours cared about her.

Let us make sure that our friends, whether elderly or not, know that we care about them and not just assume that they do. It can make all the difference.

THURSDAY—AUGUST 17.

YOUNG David had been asking his mother for a baby brother for a long time and had always been told, "Perhaps one day when we can afford one." So it was with great excitement that he rushed home one day.

"Put your coat on quickly, Mum," he said. "There's a Summer fete at the church this afternoon and it says 'Children Free'!"

FRIDAY—AUGUST 18.

WHEN Dr Albert Schweitzer was growing old, his friends and admirers sought to mark his achievements as a missionary and philosopher by building a monument to him. The site they chose was a high rock near the village of Gunsbach in Alsace, where he had spent his childhood and to which he had returned when he came home from Africa.

Schweitzer would not hear of them erecting the monument in his lifetime, but he was deeply moved and grateful, especially as the rock was a spot very dear to his heart. In his letter of thanks he wrote: "It is there I was absorbed in thought. It is there I should like to remain in stone, so that my friends can pay me a visit, devote a thought to me, and listen to the murmur of the river — the music that accompanied the movement of my own thoughts."

Today, visitors pause by the monument to remember the great humanitarian who devoted his gifts to the poor and the sick of Africa.

THE FRIENDSHIP BOOK

SATURDAY—AUGUST 19.

IT is an awesome thought that we leave all kinds of footprints as we walk through life. Some leave visible imprints, such as influence on our children's lives, but others are less obvious — for example, the prints we leave on other people's lives, perhaps through the help we give them, the jokes we pass on or words of encouragement.

We rarely think about it, but everywhere we go we all leave some kind of mark. The verse of an old and well-loved hymn sums it up like this:

Lives of good men all remind us
We can make our lives sublime,
And departing leave behind us
Footprints on the sands of time.

SUNDAY—AUGUST 20.

IT is God that girdeth me with strength, and maketh my way perfect.

Psalms 18:32

MONDAY—AUGUST 21.

A SUMMER evening quiet and still
The cattle lie contented,
The swallows skim the rippling pond
The garden air is scented.
There's music and there's laughter
With children at their play,
As the thrush sing from the briar
At the closing of the day.

Thomas Brown.

HEAVEN SCENT

THE FRIENDSHIP BOOK

TUESDAY—AUGUST 22.

I HAVE a friend with a very infectious laugh, and she always seems to use it just at the right moment. For example, if someone is out of sorts she brings about a cure with that laugh of hers.

Since I've known Evelyn I've really learned the truth of the saying: "Happiness is contagious — be a carrier". I try to be like her, but it isn't easy without that special laugh, a gift which can only belong to her.

WEDNESDAY—AUGUST 23.

THERE'S nothing I enjoy more at this glorious time of year, when days are longer than nights, than to get up early and spend an hour alone pottering in my garden. There, with only the birds for company, I can absorb the peace and quiet to prepare me for the day ahead.

Back in the 1800s, Celia Thaxter must have experienced the same feeling for she wrote: "When in these fresh mornings I go into my garden before anyone is awake, I go for the time being into perfect happiness. In this hour, divinely fresh and still, the fair face of every flower salutes me with a silent joy".

Not everyone, of course, would look on a spot of gardening as the perfect start to their day. But to give ourselves a little treat at the beginning of each new day by doing something we really enjoy, could influence our attitude for the rest of the hours ahead. I'm sure it would make us feel so much better. Why not try it, too?

THURSDAY—AUGUST 24.

I THINK the saying "a dog is man's best friend" is truer today than perhaps ever before.

Guide dogs are more than just friends to those who have lost their sight — they are a real life-line — and nowadays dogs are being trained to be living hearing-aids for the those among us who are deaf.

They bring happiness, too. Have you ever seen an official "pat dog" working in a hospice or a nursing home, creating interest and conversation? A dog in the United States was brought into a family of six children where three had been adopted. They could not seem to get on together, but the arrival of Rover did the trick — they then had one common interest.

We should always value our four-legged friends. Who knows when it will be our turn to depend on these ever-faithful companions?

FRIDAY—AUGUST 25.

WE owe our thought for today to Benjamin Franklin, the American statesman, writer and honoured man of science. Born in Boston in 1706, he died in Philadelphia in 1790, and became at the age of seventy the first Ambassador of the American Republic to France.

He wrote: "Human felicity is produced not so much by great pieces of good fortune that seldom happen, as by little advantages that occur every day."

Words to keep in mind, don't you agree?

SATURDAY—AUGUST 26.

I RECEIVED a letter from a friend one morning. One trait Beth dislikes is the tendency some people have to make rather disparaging remarks if someone has succeeded in a certain area of life.

"To speak well of others is to speak well of oneself," she wrote.

It's true, isn't it? It is easy to belittle others, but it is surely kinder and wiser to look at their merits and acknowledge their talents. Remember, we reveal a great deal about our own character in the way we talk about others.

SUNDAY—AUGUST 27.

L ET not your heart be troubled: ye believe in God, believe also in me.

John 14:1

MONDAY—AUGUST 28.

D O you ever listen to "Thought For The Day" on the radio? I certainly do. I like these short interludes in which a speaker dispenses some wise words to think about in the hours to come. It is quite remarkable how much can be said in a short time.

One contributor, the late Robert Foxcroft, put it very neatly when he said the purpose of the programme was "to keep the rumour of God alive". A good way of putting it, and isn't it amazing how quickly rumours can spread once the first whisper is uttered?

HEART TO HEART

TUESDAY—AUGUST 29.

"SOMETIMES a light surprises the Christian when he sings." Hearing these words sung in a "Songs Of Praise" programme reminded me of the Bible's account of St Paul being beaten and then imprisoned for daring to speak openly of his Christian beliefs. And we are told that when in prison he broke into song.

So if Paul used singing to help his feelings, surely the inspiration of singing can help us, too. It doesn't matter if our voices are not good — it's just that making the effort to sing will lift up our spirits, as St Paul discovered all those years ago.

WEDNESDAY—AUGUST 30.

I FOUND these words spoken by Lord Balfour, who was a Prime Minister last century:
"The best thing to give to your enemy
　　is forgiveness;
to an opponent, tolerance;
to a friend, your heart;
to your child, a good example;
to a father, deference;
to your mother, conduct that will make her
　　proud of you;
to yourself, respect;
to all men, charity".

THURSDAY—AUGUST 31.

LOVE and friendship are rich gold threads which run through the tapestry of life making it sparkle and glow with their warmth.

September

ONE sunny day, the Lady of the House and I visited a nearby town, and found the weekly market in full swing. The streets were busy with noise and bustle, traders were shouting out their wares, while shoppers were talking and laughing. All around, brightly-canopied stalls groaned under the weight of fresh fruit and vegetables; huge striped marrows and plump pumpkins jostled mounds of plums and pears and piles of crisp golden and red-cheeked apples.

As we walked around, we had to weave our way past rows of tall buckets on the ground, each crammed with flowers — salmon-pink and white carnations, sweet peas, love-in-a-mist and lily-of-the-valley, each filling the air with their distinctive perfume.

I don't usually regard this world as a drab place, but if ever I should feel tempted to, I'll simply take myself off to the nearest street market!

WE can never replace a true friend. When a man is fortunate enough to have several, he finds they are all different. No one has a double in friendship.

CUT AND DRIED

SUNDAY—SEPTEMBER 3.

THEREFORE being justified by faith, we have peace with God through our Lord Jesus Christ.

Romans 5: 1

MONDAY—SEPTEMBER 4.

"**W**HERE there is no hope there is no endeavour," wrote Dr Samuel Johnson. Yet what exactly is hope? Taking one letter at a time, we can perhaps make these suggestions:

H — An honest assessment of a situation weighing up future prospects.

O — Optimism, sister of hope, enabling us to look on the positive side of life.

P — Persistence, an attribute that helps to increase enthusiasm.

E — Endurance, knowing that if we have come through a bad patch, then hopefully later ones can be worked out successfully.

TUESDAY—SEPTEMBER 5.

A PRAYER FOR CHANGE

L ORD of all seasons,
Everything changes, nothing stays the same,
Teach me to accept this, and learn from it.
As the year changes, so, too, our lives must change.
Let me keep in my heart, the hope of Spring,
And the glory of Autumn.
In this ever-changing world,
Lord, let me always be aware of Your love,
For this alone is everlasting, unfailing,
And unchangeable – Amen.

WEDNESDAY—SEPTEMBER 6.

HOW we all blossom with a little bit of encouragement!

I heard about a schoolboy who had been taking part in his school sports day and wasn't doing very well. All his friends had won their events and, as they watched him lagging behind, they said, "Come on, let's give Ken a cheer to help him along." So they cheered and called out encouragingly to their friend who, by putting on an extra spurt, managed to be first past the winning post.

In "The Evening Gull" Derek Tangye wrote: "If a person is in trouble, lift them up. Make the person feel fine, feel good. Never yield to the temptation of pointing out a fault. Such a fault, however trivial, becomes hurtfully exaggerated in the person's mind."

If we can inspire somebody with the confidence to do something, let's not neglect the opportunity, for there's no telling where it might lead!

THURSDAY—SEPTEMBER 7.

WHEN we count our many blessings,
It isn't hard to see
That what we value most in life
Are the treasures that are free.
For it's not the things that we possess
That signify our wealth,
But the blessings that are priceless
Like our family, friends and health.

Olive Beazley-Long.

FRIDAY—SEPTEMBER 8.

SOMEONE once said: "Marriage is an institution and not everybody wants to live in an institution." A cynical statement, certainly, but there are many more positive points of view as the following quotations illustrate:

A successful marriage requires falling in love many times — with the same person.

Marriage is a deal in which a man gives away half his groceries in order to get the other half cooked. (Of course, there is a more enlightened way of expressing that by saying, "Marriage is a matter of give and take".)

G. K. Chesterton described the strength of marriage when he called it "an armed alliance against the outside world". An alliance which will often win through, in spite of adversity and the hard knocks we have to face.

SATURDAY—SEPTEMBER 9.

I'D like to share these quotes from my collection with you today:

Silence is not only golden, it is seldom misquoted!

Busy souls have no time to be busybodies.

SUNDAY—SEPTEMBER 10.

COME now, and let us reason together, saith the Lord: though your sins be as scarlet, they shall be as white as snow.

Isaiah 1:18

THE FRIENDSHIP BOOK

WHEN the Para-Olympics were started, the chairman in his opening speech to the disabled athletes said: "It's not what you've lost but what you have that matters."

My goodness, these words don't only apply to those particular athletes. What a difference it would make to our own life, and that of others around us, if we could stop bemoaning losses, the past, and simply make the best of the present.

We'd be so much happier if we tried to act upon this. It's worth trying today — and tomorrow — don't you think?

ON a bright September afternoon, and in a burst of enthusiasm, I decided to make a start on reorganising my herbaceous border. It had become overcrowded and the flowers hadn't produced the fine show I had hoped for.

However, when I was digging among the plants I saw that the roots had become choked with bindweed and couch grass. No wonder they were struggling! Later, as I replanted them carefully in good, cleaned earth, I felt I was giving them every chance to flourish during the next season.

How like life, I thought. So often we get in a tangle with things that mar our relationships — misunderstandings, impatience and envy, to name three. Just as in the garden, it's best to root them out in the early stages and make a fresh start.

THE FRIENDSHIP BOOK

WEDNESDAY—SEPTEMBER 13.

"HAPPINESS," a rather pompous speaker once declared, "comes from the pursuit of something, not the catching of it."

"You've never chased the last bus on a wet night!" called out a loud voice from the back of the hall.

THURSDAY—SEPTEMBER 14.

I WAS interested to hear about the lady who regretted she was unable to gather the scent from her favourite flowers and bottle it, so that she could enjoy their perfume for ever. It is one of the few things that cannot be preserved — but others can.

Lavender that has been so fragrant in the flower beds in Summer can be dried and used to perfume drawers, cushions and linen cupboards; fruit from the garden can be made into jam; batches of home-made cakes can be put into the depths of the freezer for our future enjoyment. Nowadays, too, we can video our favourite films and television programmes and then we have the pleasure of watching them once again whenever we choose.

And what about our memories? Like the lavender from a Summer's garden, they will remain fresh and fragrant if we gather them and preserve them.

Blessed indeed is the person who can rejoice in happy recollections when skies are grey.

FRIDAY—SEPTEMBER 15.

I DON'T know who first said it, but I like this thought which I saw pinned to a noticeboard in a hostel for the homeless:

"If every man would mend a man, then all the world would be mended."

SATURDAY—SEPTEMBER 16.

WHEN I first read this poem called "Willing Hands" I thought that it contained some lovely thoughts and I'm sure you'll agree:

It's willing hands that catch us,
When we fear that we might fall.
It's willing hands that guide us,
Throughout our lives, over all.

It's willing hands that soothe us,
When we are full of woe.
It's willing hands that lead us,
Over rugged paths, you know.

These willing hands are hidden,
Hands we'll never see,
But God's willing hands are with us,
No matter where we be.

Glenda Moore.

SUNDAY—SEPTEMBER 17.

THEREFORE I will look unto the Lord; I will wait for the God of my salvation: my God will hear me.

Micah 7:7

MONDAY—SEPTEMBER 18.

IT was Harvest Festival time and a teacher had taken her class to the church next door which had been decorated for the annual service.

Back in the classroom they discussed what the children had seen that wasn't usually found in church, and hands shot up as they mentioned sheaves of corn, runner beans, peas, turnips and potatoes and so on.

"And can anyone think of one word to cover all these things?" asked the teacher.

"Yes, Miss," said an eager young lad. "Gravy."

TUESDAY—SEPTEMBER 19.

HARRIET BEECHER STOWE of the United States and William Wilberforce of England had something in common — they both declared war on slavery. Women in Harriet's society could not stand up and speak, so the only weapon she had was her pen. She wrote a famous book, "Uncle Tom's Cabin", which contributed to the eventual abolition of slavery in the United States.

William Wilberforce was a Christian member of parliament in England, and argued for abolition of the slave trade in the British Empire. He failed many times, but in the end saw his dream come true. An act of parliament was passed in the House of Commons to abolish slavery.

These two people started a task which seemed impossible — yet both won through. Now, if we all used our gifts for a good cause, there is no telling what we could do in our own generation.

SUNSET SONG

WEDNESDAY—SEPTEMBER 20.

CHELMORTON is one of the highest villages in Derbyshire, and sees more than its share of snow, mists and rain. When we were last there we spoke to a resident who told us this story.

A lady, who once kept the village store, was a devout Methodist, and a room at the back of the shop was used for worship as there was no local chapel. She was thrilled when she heard that the famous John Wesley was coming to preach. The day at last arrived but it was atrocious weather.

She knew that Wesley was risking life and limb to arrive at the village across dark and lonely countryside, so she bravely set off with a lantern to meet and guide him safely. Wesley himself had often done just this for many a lost soul in a dark place. He had held high the lantern of Christian truth — and so did this stranger.

THURSDAY—SEPTEMBER 21.

A RECEPTIONIST was explaining to a patient how much care had gone into redecorating the doctor's practice. It had been decided to paint the waiting-room in different shades of green because it was felt that the effect would be soothing for those waiting to see the doctor.

One of the other patients, looking through the window towards a beautiful panorama of hills and fields ringed by leafy trees, remarked, "I think God discovered that long ago".

Indeed, what can be more calming than a walk through the countryside?

FRIDAY—SEPTEMBER 22.

ONE day, a sudden breeze blew through an open window, riffling the paper on which I was writing, but thanks to my paperweight the sheets placed alongside stayed put. I looked at the paperweight — just an ordinary glass one brought back as a holiday souvenir.

John Ruskin, the famous 19th-century writer and critic, had a beautiful stone paperweight on which was carved the word "today". He took this as his personal motto — the word being a constant reminder that each day was a gift from God, to be used joyfully, faithfully and usefully.

A good motto for us all, don't you think? After all, we can't do much about the past once it has gone but if we live today as best we can, then surely that is the best preparation for tomorrow.

SATURDAY—SEPTEMBER 23.

I'VE chosen these quotes from my scrapbook for you to think about today:

Beauty and wonder, love and kindness — glimpses of Heaven, here on earth.

Each day is a new adventure, so step out bravely and catch the sunshine on the way.

SUNDAY—SEPTEMBER 24.

THY word is a lamp unto my feet, and a light unto my path.

Psalms 119: 105

MONDAY—SEPTEMBER 25.

THE Lady of the House was once unable to have her usual kind of hair-do. The stylist explained that the hood dryer was out of order and she would have to use a hand dryer instead.

However, all was well on her next visit and she asked what the problem had been. "Oh," said Sally, "it was just one small wire which had become disconnected." What a lot of bother had been caused. It put me in mind of that old rhyme:

For want of a nail the shoe was lost,
For want of a shoe the horse was lost,
For want of a horse the rider was lost,
For want of a rider the battle was lost,
And all for want of a horse-shoe nail.

Yes, often we are more dependent on the small things of life than we realise.

TUESDAY—SEPTEMBER 26.

AUTUMN

THE Autumn comes swiftly, with russet
and red,
With ragged clouds racing over my head,
The silver birch bending, the wind growing cold
And rustling carpets of yellow and gold.
Remember September, she leaves a warm glow,
And golden October, a magical show,
Though Winter comes creeping, don't let it
dismay,
Keep Autumn within you, to brighten each day.

Iris Hesselden.

THE FRIENDSHIP BOOK

WEDNESDAY—SEPTEMBER 27.

WHEN Miss Betty Boothroyd M.P. was elected Speaker of the House of Commons it proved a popular choice. Such a high position demanded just those qualities of firmness and fairness she had always shown and, of course, sound speaking abilities. She also has a fine sense of humour and can enjoy a joke against herself as an after-dinner speech once revealed.

In her early days she was invited to address the annual gathering at a local voluntary organisation. Though nervous, she got through her speech and was well received then later, was asked if she wanted any expenses. She replied that after such a pleasant evening there was no fee.

"That's very kind of you," said the secretary. "You see, we are a new organisation and busy saving up for a first-class speaker next year!"

THURSDAY—SEPTEMBER 28.

THERE'S a tree at our primary school gates which has a "lucky hole" in its trunk. No-one knows how it got there, but they do know why it is called the "lucky hole" . . . because all manner of things to delight small children are found in it — perhaps a few marbles, small toys or sweets.

That "lucky tree" gives pleasure to young and old. Many mothers, fathers and grandparents pass the spot but they are careful not to be seen popping little things into the trunk. You see, that would spoil the surprise, for it is surely such acts of thoughtfulness which make life so special.

FRIDAY—SEPTEMBER 29.

DO you know the story of Brother Anselm? He was a pious monk who studied the Scriptures daily, and was devoted to silent prayer. His fellow monks respected his learning, although most of them worked in the garden and the kitchen, also caring for the sick.

One day, Brother Anselm visited a distant monastery, to study in the library there, and soon made the monks feel that he was above their mundane tasks. But the wise old Abbot had a surprise in store. When the call to supper came, Brother Anselm, studying manuscripts in his cell as usual, was not disturbed. Then, when he heard the other monks preparing for their last prayers of the day, he rushed out and asked the Abbot indignantly why he had not been called to supper.

"We thought prayer and study were meat and drink sufficient for you," replied the Abbot with apparent surprise.

There is indeed a time to study and to pray; and there is also a time to lend a hand elsewhere.

SATURDAY—SEPTEMBER 30.

IT'S wise, now and then, to remind ourselves that man does not know it all. That brilliant mind, Albert Schweitzer, put it this way:

"As we acquire more knowledge, things do not become more comprehensible, but more mysterious."

October

AND the Lord shall be king over all the earth: in that day shall there be one Lord, and his name one.

Zechariah 14:9

NOT long ago we had a visit from our newly-retired friends Isabel and Robin. For many years they had worked long hours in a small shop and post office.

Over a cup of tea Isabel told us, "Robin and I loved the busy coming and going at the shop, but latterly we both found ourselves saying that one day when we had time we'd do this or that, but the problem was we couldn't ever find the time, so we decided to retire a little early."

Robin agreed. "Now we plan to do all those things we spoke about. Nothing very grand, you know, just going away for the day when the weather is fine, spending more time with our family and friends, and Isabel will have more time for her favourite charity, while I will be able to work in the garden."

Robin and Isabel are over 60, but they're going places — their places — and isn't that what the best retirements are all about?

TUESDAY—OCTOBER 3.

LEGEND says that the first chrysanthemum was created by a Chinese bride-to-be who had been told that her marriage would last for as many years as the petals on the flower on her wedding dress.

She found a flower with 17 petals and carefully divided each petal into two, then four. Her marriage lasted 68 wonderful years.

A lovely story about a lovely flower.

WEDNESDAY—OCTOBER 4.

ELIZABETH, a friend of ours, takes great pleasure in visiting old churches, and over the years has travelled many miles to see them. I congratulated her on her unflagging enthusiasm.

"I'm certainly enthusiastic," she agreed, "but not quite unflagging." With a twinkle in her eye, she showed me a verse she had written after a visit to an ancient abbey:

By the tomb, an angel kneels,
Serene in her marble gown.
She's held the pose for a thousand years,
And still she makes no frown.
Her naked feet are cold and white,
Her hands are stiff in prayer,
And yet her face is calm, and holds
No hint of worldly care.
So why can't I, whose visit here,
Is only a one-day treat,
Think, like her, of heavenly bliss,
Instead of my aching feet?

THURSDAY—OCTOBER 5.

EVERY morning on his way to work Roy used to pass traffic lights where there were always long delays. Everyone got impatient, waiting for their turn to go their different ways. While waiting one wet morning, he had a brainwave.

There was a restaurant nearby called "Back In Time". It had a clock outside going round and round backwards very quickly.

Still watching the cars in front and behind, Roy decided that it would probably help to pass the time if he, too, went back in time. He saw himself in his mind's eye as a boy paddling in the sea and playing on the sands with his family. Then he visualised sunsets, waterfalls and the moon shining on snow, a quiet stream flowing through a field of golden buttercups.

After this "mental holiday", Roy arrived at work feeling remarkably calm and happy. It is wonderful to find contentment within ourselves, an oasis of tranquillity.

FRIDAY—OCTOBER 6.

ON looking back we ponder
On the things that we have done,
And we sometimes wonder
How the race is run.
For life's a game of pitch and toss
We can't win all the way,
Don't count the cost if you have lost —
You'll win another day!

Dorothy M. Loughran.

SATURDAY—OCTOBER 7.

WILLIAM COWPER'S mother died when he was six, he was bullied at school and for much of his life suffered from mental illness.

Despite all this, he wrote two of the most comforting hymns in the English language, "God Moves In A Mysterious Way" and "O For A Closer Walk With God", as well as that great humorous poem, "John Gilpin".

It is a sign of his greatness that there is no hint of his own troubles in the works we remember him by.

SUNDAY—OCTOBER 8.

FOR with thee is the fountain of life: in thy light shall we see light.

Psalms 36:9

MONDAY—OCTOBER 9.

HAVE you ever come across those lines written by George Pettie in the late 16th century? I have kept the old spellings.

"True friends are not like new garments which be the worse for wearing: they are rather like the stoane of Scilcia, which the more it is beaten the harder it is, or like spices, which the more they are pounded, the sweeter they are; or like many wines, which the older they are the better they are".

How true these lines are today as yesterday, don't you agree? Where would we be without friendship, tried and tested, which survives the ups and downs of life?

TUESDAY—OCTOBER 10.

ON the walls of South Stoke Church in Sussex there is this "Common Sense Prayer" which draws the attention of visitors who enter to admire its attractive interior:

Give me a good digestion, Lord;
And something to digest.
Give me a healthy body, Lord,
And sense to keep it at its best.
Give me a healthy mind, O Lord,
To keep the good and pure in sight
Which seeing sin is not appalled;
But finds a way to put it right.
Give me a mind that is not bored
That does not whimper, whine or sigh,
Don't let me worry overmuch about
This funny thing called I.
Give me a sense of humour, Lord,
The grace to see a joke.
To get some happiness from life and
Pass it on to other folk.

WEDNESDAY—OCTOBER 11.

WHEN I was leafing through a scrapbook of quotations I came across these lines and think they're worth passing on.

Birthdays are just like buses,
At first they take for ever,
Then the moment your back is turned,
They all arrive together!

Anon.

HAPPY WANDERERS

THURSDAY—OCTOBER 12.

AFTER a busy day, there is nothing the Lady of the House and I enjoy more than relaxing in a comfortable chair, sipping tea and listening to our favourite music. It never fails to refresh us when we feel too tired to do anything else.

As long ago as 400 B.C. Plato wrote: "Music and rhythm find their way into the secret places of the soul," while Sydney Smith put it this way: "Music . . . the only cheap and unpunished rapture upon earth."

I once came across a musician's prayer written by Alvin O. Langdon: "This is my prayer . . . that the impressions I make on the white pages of manuscript may encourage, cheer and inspire all those who hear my song; that I may write together in my own life all those major chords that make for happy, creative, triumphant living."

What a great deal we have to be thankful for where music is concerned. "It touches every key of memory," wrote Belle Brittain. "I love it for what it makes me forget . . . and for what it makes me remember."

FRIDAY—OCTOBER 13.

I KNOW he has his troubles like us all, but he smiles a lot, real, genuine smiles, the man I am thinking of. Graham is cheerful and optimistic, with a friendly word for all.

"Francis," he said to me, "I like to keep life sunny side up!"

Good for him — let's follow his example!

SATURDAY—OCTOBER 14.

MY friend Ron is head of a village school, and he asked me to call in one day to see the children. I've no doubt he is proud of his young pupils and wanted to show them off. The school is a church school so I was not surprised to find one class writing on the theme "God is love".

I decided to make a note of some of the thoughts the youngsters had written:

"I've felt God's love when I was playing with my friends. It made me feel all warm inside."

"God loves everyone. It doesn't matter if we're black, blue, green or orange."

"God may only have two ears, but He can still hear everyone's prayer."

"If people are new to school I'll be their friend."

Children are our future and it is comforting to think that with the love and compassion these children show for those around them, there is plenty of hope.

SUNDAY—OCTOBER 15.

LET all things be done decently and in order.

Corinthians I 14:40

MONDAY—OCTOBER 16.

A STRANGER entering a church was handed a rather battered Bible. "I'm sorry," said the man on the door, "but they're all like that."

"Don't apologise," said the stranger. "If the Bibles are falling apart, it shows that your congregation isn't!"

TUESDAY—OCTOBER 17.

WHEN Nancy injured her leg it took a long time to heal and she had to use crutches to get about. For someone who had been used to rushing around, the process seemed very slow indeed. One of her friends said that she would pray for her to make a swift recovery.

Nancy replied, "No, just pray for God to give me patience."

How much more worthwhile to pray that we may withstand life's difficulties rather than try to avoid them altogether!

WEDNESDAY—OCTOBER 18.

A YOUNG friend of ours, Neil, had to move to London after he was promoted and was looking forward to it all with excitement and understandably, some trepidation.

Once he was settled we had a long letter from him. He told us that when he had first arrived, his taxi driver soon saw that he did not really know his way around, and had found accommodation for him that night with his sister.

It seems that a friend from the church he joined soon helped him to find a flat. London can be rather impersonal, as all large cities can be, yet here was Neil writing and telling us: "My experiences so far have taught me that it is not so much the place that counts — but the people."

We should all try to make our towns, streets, churches and homes more friendly because after all, "It's the people in them who count."

THURSDAY—OCTOBER 19.

"THAT wretched phone again!" grumbled our friend Jack. "Three times today I've been dragged indoors to answer it, and for what? A wrong number, then people trying to sell their products."

Like all inventions, the phone has its pros and cons and here is a heart-warming tale for us to share. It was the first anniversary of our friend Jill's husband's death. A sad day, and Jill had no family nearby to share the hours with, her only daughter living abroad.

Then her phone rang. "Hi, Mum!" said the voice of her beloved Laura. "Just to let you know we're all thinking of you today. Now listen, here's your granddaughter Sarah to send you a special message."

Over the air sounded a series of gurgles, with a few bumps as a tiny four-month-old fist knocked against the receiver. How Jill laughed, even as the tears overflowed. But this time the tears were not bitter and lonely, for they sprang from love.

Now, do you know of anyone who'd like to hear a friendly voice on the line today?

FRIDAY—OCTOBER 20.

ARE you good at being idle? The humorous writer Jerome K. Jerome wrote a book entitled "Idle Thoughts Of An Idle Fellow", but in it he admits: "It is impossible to enjoy idling thoroughly unless one has plenty of work to do!"

SATURDAY—OCTOBER 21.

PRAYER FOR COURAGE

*LORD, give me courage this I pray
To face each new awakening day,
Without it I can only be
A phantom ship upon life's sea.*

*When sorrow arises, help me find
Through courage, happy peace of mind.
If tears be shed, then let them be
Foretaste of heart's tranquillity.*

Georgina Hall.

SUNDAY—OCTOBER 22.

FOR I am not ashamed of the gospel of Christ: for it is the power of God unto salvation to every one that believeth.

Romans 1:16

MONDAY—OCTOBER 23.

"WHENEVER Sarah comes into our house, she seems to leave behind her a truly delightful fragrance," said a neighbour.

No, Sarah doesn't use expensive perfume! It is a fragrance of the spirit that was referred to, for never once is Sarah heard to gossip unkindly; instead the goodness within human nature, and above all, the ministry of Christ, are the main topics of her conversation. Not preached, but just talked about in a natural kind of way.

Now, I wonder what sort of "fragrance" I leave behind in any house I visit.

TUESDAY—OCTOBER 24.

I HEARD a story one day about a seaside tea-room which was filled with holidaymakers. Suddenly, the waitress rushed to the door and shouted, "I've got a rat!"

Consternation spread throughout the room as mothers hastily picked up their children and people looked unhappily at their plates of half-eaten food. However, panic began to subside as the waitress waved a child's sun-bonnet high in the air to attract the attention of a departing family. What she had, in fact, said was: "I've got her hat."

How easy it is for misunderstandings to arise; then feelings get hurt and relationships are spoiled through a few careless words. Let us try to be sure that all our misunderstandings are as quickly put right as the one in the tea-room.

WEDNESDAY—OCTOBER 25.

D AG Hammarskjold, the much-loved UN Secretary General who died in a plane crash in 1961, used to say this simple prayer and I'd like to pass it on to you:

"Night is drawing nigh. For all that has been, thanks. For all that shall be, thanks."

THURSDAY—OCTOBER 26.

I N a church near us the collection is taken during the service. One day a small girl was heard to say, "Look, Mummy, there's a man coming to collect the fares!"

FRIDAY—OCTOBER 27.

GEOFFREY SMITH, formerly the superintendent of the lovely Harlow Gardens at Harrogate, is perhaps best remembered for his gardening programmes. When he went to live in the Yorkshire Dales he said, "There will be no more television series. I'll settle for what I have."

One time he joined Alan Titchmarsh in the "Sweet Inspiration" television programme in which he spoke about hymns which had inspired him. He said, "I shall never forget how precious beautiful things are. When I want reassurance that under all the turmoil the world is still all right, I return to the small village in Wensleydale where I was born. That puts everything in perspective."

He told a story about the day he bought a field. The farmer he bid against asked what he intended doing with it.

"I plan to plant gorse and sit and look at it," said Geoffrey.

"You're mad," said the farmer.

"It's a very splendid form of madness though, isn't it?" replied Geoffrey.

That's something worth considering!

SATURDAY—OCTOBER 28.

A YOUNG Indian student once wrote to a missionary friend who had gone home to England. Trying to find the right phrase to finish off, he looked up the dictionary. The missionary was surprised to read: "May the Lord pickle you", instead of "May the Lord preserve you"!

SUNDAY—OCTOBER 29.

JESUS saith unto him, I am the way, the truth, and the life: no man cometh unto the Father, but by me.

John 14:6

MONDAY—OCTOBER 30.

I WAS once given a book of verse. On the fly-leaf was written an ancient blessing: "May you live a hundred warm summers."

I was reminded of this not long ago when an old lady in the village died, aged one hundred and one. Patricia had worked hard all her life. As a young girl, in Ireland, she had toiled in the potato fields, often carrying heavy bags on her back, sometimes rowing across a lough with another heavy load. Her father had been a gamekeeper so, on occasion, they had been privileged to share some of the special events on the estate.

When we attended Patricia's 100th birthday celebrations she talked of those times, many years ago. She remembered the long Summer days of her youth. Forgotten were the cold Winters and all the sad times. What an example to us all!

May you, too, live a hundred warm Summers!

TUESDAY—OCTOBER 31.

THE writer Charles Kingsley once told an audience not to be afraid of looking too happy. "Don't think," he said, "that you honour God by wearing a sour face when He is heaping blessings upon you, and calling on you to smile and sing."

November

WEDNESDAY—NOVEMBER 1.

THE Lady of the House and I were so pleased to hear that two friends of ours had settled their differences after a quarrel. We were sure it had all been a bit of a storm in a tea-cup, a silly misunderstanding, when two rather nice but cross people had said things they didn't really mean to each other, and had then parted in a huff.

Then one day one of the people concerned picked up the phone, dialled through and said: "Hello, Fred, it's Andrew! Haven't seen you for ages, so how about meeting up?"

Fred replied, "All right, let's do that. Since I last saw you, I've often wanted to get in touch but was afraid you wouldn't want to speak to me after we'd had words."

Don't fear a rebuff, or be too proud to take the first step to heal a quarrel, or mend a break in friendship.

THURSDAY—NOVEMBER 2.

I LIKE the wish that the writer Jonathan Swift sent to a friend: "May you live all the days of your life." It reminds me of another saying, by the boxer, Joe E. Louis: "You only live once — but if you work it right, once is enough."

FRIDAY—NOVEMBER 3.

AFTER many years as a Sunday school teacher, Marjorie was retiring, so the Lady of the House and I went along to the party given in her honour. The verbal tributes were as plentiful as the flowers and presents, and afterwards I asked what advice she would give to anyone just starting the job.

Marjorie looked thoughtful. "Well," she said, "I suppose the most important thing is always try to be kind. I'm afraid," she admitted, "that I never found it possible to love all my pupils, but it was always possible to be kind. And, do you know," she added with a smile, "it's amazing how often a little kindness made them loveable."

I'm sure Marjorie will be sadly missed from our Sunday school — and how many lives she has enriched while she was there!

SATURDAY—NOVEMBER 4.

IT needs thinking about but I have long treasured these words by the American author and preacher, Henry Ward Beecher. He once said:

"In this world it is not what we *take* up, but what we *give* up, that makes us rich."

SUNDAY—NOVEMBER 5.

THE Lord is good, a strong hold in the day of trouble; and he knoweth them that trust in him.

Nahum 1:7

THE FRIENDSHIP BOOK

MONDAY—NOVEMBER 6.

TRACY set off with her mother for her first day at a new school in great excitement, but as soon as they had crossed the street with the lollipop lady she burst into tears. At last her mother found out what the matter was.

Tracy had thought the lollipop lady was a woman who handed out lollipops!

TUESDAY—NOVEMBER 7.

ON arriving home, Janice found on her doorstep a magnificent bouquet of flowers, beautifully wrapped and tied with golden ribbon. Thrilled, she searched for the card, only to find that although the bouquet had her street name on it, the surname was not hers! It should have been delivered to a couple who lived a few doors away.

She looked longingly at that magnificent bouquet — how it would have brightened up her home on this dreary Winter's day — but of course Janice promptly delivered the flowers to the correct address.

The next day she found a pot-plant on her doorstep — an African violet in full bloom accompanied by a simple card: "Thank you for delivering our Golden Wedding bouquet". The sight of the magnificent blooms on her doorstep had originally given Janice a glow, but it didn't feel nearly as satisfying as the warmth she felt on receiving the unexpected gift — one meant just for her.

CAPITAL COLOUR

WEDNESDAY—NOVEMBER 8.

I FOUND these prayers in a church magazine, giving two different views of the same problem. First came a motorist's prayer:

"Lord, help me to drive with a steady hand, a sure eye, and good control, so that I will not bring any harm to others. Teach me to be a responsible driver, and curb my desire for excessive speed. May the beauty of the world you have created always accompany me on my travels."

Then there followed a much shorter pedestrian's prayer:

"Lord, just let me get across the road in one piece!"

I could not help thinking that these different appeals could be made by just one simple prayer for all:

"Please let me remember the other person and give him or her due consideration."

THURSDAY—NOVEMBER 9.

WINTER

THOUGH Winter winds are blowing chill,
Our memories can warm us still,
And evenings have a special glow,
Outshining fog and frost or snow.
A time of friendship, love and cheer,
To carry with us through the year,
And soon we'll see dark days depart,
And Springtime lift each waiting heart.

Iris Hesselden.

FRIDAY—NOVEMBER 10.

SHAKESPEARE wrote in his play "All's Well That Ends Well" — "The web of our life is of mingled yarn, good and ill together".

How true, but isn't that what makes life so fascinating?

SATURDAY—NOVEMBER 11.

NOWADAYS, we are fortunate in having a rich variety of hymns to accompany our worship, from the traditional "Hymns Ancient And Modern" to the newest choruses which are popular.

This was not the case when Issac Watts was born in 1674. When he was twenty years old, he complained that the hymns sung at his chapel were of very poor quality. His father, a deacon, was shocked and challenged his son to produce something better.

Isaac took him at his word and, over the next two years, he composed a new hymn for every Sunday service. We remember him today for such memorable hymns as "When I Survey The Wondrous Cross" and "O God Our Help In Ages Past".

These are among the words of Isaac Watts that have given comfort and inspiration:

Awake our souls! Away, our fears!
Let every trembling thought be gone!
Awake, and run the heavenly race,
And put a cheerful courage on.

THE FRIENDSHIP BOOK

SING praises to the Lord, which dwelleth in Zion: declare among the people his doings.

Psalms 9:11

IF only I was slim, Dawn cried,
  Ignoring her kind heart inside,
Her lovely hair, her silky skin,
  She only wished that she was thin.

These awful lines make me look old
  Another cried, whose heart was gold,
Her gentle face and blue-eyed twinkle,
  Have lost their fight with many a wrinkle.

Fiona's legs were long, her figure great,
  But her straight hair was her pet hate,
Though she was beautiful and fair,
  She wished that she had curly hair.

Not satisfied, we want the lot,
  Not grateful for the things we've got,
But none of these should cause us pride —
  Real beauty is what's there inside.
                    Chrissy Greenslade.

TAKE this tip where e'er you go —
  Keep hopes high, but woe quite low.
                    J. M. Robertson.

WEDNESDAY—NOVEMBER 15.

I SUPPOSE the one thing everybody in this world seeks is happiness. Here is just one recipe, given by Yves Printemps:

"To be happy you should have something to do, someone to love, and something to hope for."

THURSDAY—NOVEMBER 16.

FOR many years writers have on occasion referred to life as a journey. Perhaps my favourite description, however, was given to me by an old friend, Florence, who compared her life to a train journey.

She had passed, she said, through many lonely and deserted stations along the way. Sometimes, there had been platforms which were crowded with passengers — people she already knew, and strangers who quickly became close travelling companions.

Along the way there had been dark tunnels, but beyond them, sunlight and blue skies. At other times she had thought that there was a fault on the points, or that the signals were wrong. However, her train kept moving and was never derailed.

Now, as she gets older, Florence feels the train gathering speed. Unafraid, as she has always been, she looks forward to reaching her destination; certain that those she loved and lost will be waiting to meet her.

I hope that we, also, may have such courage to help us as we travel along life's track.

FRIDAY—NOVEMBER 17.

A STORY which the Lady of the House and I like to hear is the one about Edith's missionary card. When she was small all the children in her Sunday school class were issued with such a card, and asked to see how much they could collect from friends and relatives.

She thought she would start with Grandfather but he wasn't immediately forthcoming. "You start collecting and for every pound you gather I will give you another pound!" So Edith started collecting for all she was worth.

She managed to collect six pounds, and Grandfather gave her another six. She said, "You might as well have given it to me in the first place, Grandpa."

"Not at all," he replied. "I gave you something far more important. I gave you a goal to aim for, and I'm sure you worked that much harder to reach it."

Perhaps we all need a goal to encourage us to do our very best.

SATURDAY—NOVEMBER 18.

L OVE, hope, wisdom, friendship — all are great gifts. But the greatest by far is love.

SUNDAY—NOVEMBER 19.

H EAL me, O Lord, and I shall be healed; save me, and I shall be saved: for thou art my praise.

Jeremiah 17:14

MONDAY—NOVEMBER 20.

FOR many years two ladies who had a great love of theatre, used to hold rehearsals for their young charges in a rather run-down church hall. Making sure the children could be heard was always a problem.

"Now, remember to speak up," said one, "because my Granny's sitting right at the back and she's a little hard of hearing."

What she didn't expect was this quick retort. "Well, why doesn't your Granny just come and sit at the front?"

TUESDAY—NOVEMBER 21.

THE third Tuesday in every November is World Hello Day. Since 1973, this has been an annual initiative towards peace, organised by two American brothers, Michael and Brian McCormack, who felt the importance of personal communication in the search for peace and its preservation.

Anyone can take part — and all that World Hello Day basically requires is everyone to greet ten different individuals. It doesn't have to be confined to the third Tuesday in November, either. Why not make a point of saying "Hello" to somebody every day?

A word of encouragement, a cheerful greeting can often do wonders for a lonely or preoccupied person. Sometimes it's as simple as giving a warm greeting to someone we haven't met before and may never meet again.

THE FRIENDSHIP BOOK

WEDNESDAY—NOVEMBER 22.

IF you enjoy wildlife programmes, you may have seen one about the meerkats in a series produced by Sir David Attenborough. It first appeared a number of years ago, but these small animals made such an impression that it has been repeated more than once.

The meerkat is a species of mongoose which lives in South Africa's Kalahari Desert. It is not much bigger than the tassle of a lion's tail, yet in terms of teamwork and support for those of its kind, it can teach us a thing or two.

Only by working as a team can the meerkats survive the desert, so sentinels keep careful guard while the remainder hunt for food. At the very first sign of danger, warning is given, and the community returns to safety. An endearing habit of these little animals is the way they look after the babies so vigilantly — not necessarily their own — and the strongest will always make time to groom the weakest.

In the sociability scale "Meerkats United" could rate as the top team, their motto "All for one, and one for all", an attitude which is well worth cultivating!

THURSDAY—NOVEMBER 23.

HERE is a prayer we can all use: "Make the old tolerant, the young sympathetic, the great humble, the busy patient. Make happy folk thoughtful, the clever kindly, the good pleasant, and, dear Lord, make me what I ought to be."

FRIDAY—NOVEMBER 24.

WHEN Henry Trengrouse was a young man in Helston, Cornwall, he witnessed a terrible disaster in which a ship was wrecked in a storm with the loss of about 100 lives. Afterwards, he couldn't get out of his mind how he and others had watched helplessly as the vessel sank offshore. If only, he thought, it had been possible to bridge that terrible gap.

Some time later he was watching a fireworks display. As the rockets shot into the air, he suddenly realised they were the answer.

Henry began a long series of experiments which resulted in his "Rocket Life Saving Apparatus", demonstrated in 1816. He showed how a rocket fired from a musket could shoot a light line on to a distressed ship. Once the line was secured on deck, a heavier rope could be hauled aboard and those in danger brought ashore.

It was to be a long time before the rocket came into regular use, and Henry himself received little credit or reward, but how proud he would have been to know that his invention has been responsible for saving countless lives.

SATURDAY—NOVEMBER 25.

ROBERT BROWNING wrote about a man who was "fit for the sunshine, so it followed him", while a fellow poet, William Wordsworth, described someone as "of cheerful yesterdays and confident tomorrows".

How good to be remembered that way . . .

SUNDAY—NOVEMBER 26.

HE that hath received his testimony hath set to his seal that God is true.

John 3:33

MONDAY—NOVEMBER 27.

THIS verse was seen in Grasmere Methodist Church:

If after church you wait awhile,
Someone may greet you with a smile.
But, if you quickly rise and flee
We'll all seem cold and stiff, maybe.
The one beside you in the pew
Is perhaps a stranger, too.
All here, like you, have fears and cares,
All of us need each other's prayers,
In fellowship we bid you meet,
With us around God's mercy seat.

TUESDAY—NOVEMBER 28.

THE Lady of the House was delighted with her birthday cards and gifts last year. A present which still gives her great pleasure is a tiny book of quotations connected with birthdays. One section is headed "Celebrating Your Life" and this made me pause and think.

I know we all have problems, but looking back over the years, what do we remember most clearly? Isn't it always the happy times, the love given and received and the joy of sharing?

Birthdays are certainly special occasions, but we don't need one particular day to celebrate life. We can do that every day!

THE FRIENDSHIP BOOK

WEDNESDAY—NOVEMBER 29.

THE clock is always ticking,
  The hands are moving slow,
And yet it is surprising
  How fast the hours go.
And when the hours turn to days
  The weeks are passing by,
It seems that time has sprouted wings
  As the years begin to fly.
Each precious moment of our lives
  Is changed from "now" to "then",
Offered to us only once —
  And never comes again.

Ann Rutherford.

THURSDAY—NOVEMBER 30.

SOME years ago when on holiday, I enjoyed walking around the grounds of Dunkeld Cathedral in Perthshire, at a time of day when the sun was rising beyond the wooded shoulders of Birnam Hill. The cathedral stands in its own grounds near the town — only the sound of the nearby River Tay broke the silence around me that day.

As I gazed upon the cathedral's magnificent architecture, the steeple almost, it seemed, moving against the passing clouds and the first rays of the sun etched against those ancient walls, I somehow felt as if I was not alone. These words from Psalms 19, seemed particularly relevant:

"The heavens declare the glory of God; and the firmament sheweth His handywork."

December

HOW I enjoy going on holiday and having the leisure to enjoy a full-scale breakfast! One time, as I was munching my cornflakes, followed by bacon, sausage, egg, toast and coffee, I reflected on the vast number of unknown people who had a share in providing my one breakfast.

There were the workers on the land who grew grain and harvested it for my cereal and bread; coffee and tea growers working far away in the hot sun; pig, poultry and dairy farmers nearer home, as well as transport workers and shop assistants to deliver and distribute food. Last, but not least, there was the chef who had prepared my much-appreciated breakfast.

It reminded me that we are not the self-sufficient creatures we may imagine ourselves to be, but are dependent on one another for so many things. As John Donne put it: "No man is an island . . ."

*F*RIENDSHIP *is a golden thread*
That runs throughout the years,
Look back on all the days gone by
And rejoice as that golden thread appears.

THE FRIENDSHIP BOOK

SUNDAY—DECEMBER 3.

BLESSED are the peacemakers: for they shall be called the children of God.

Matthew 5:9

MONDAY—DECEMBER 4.

A PRAYER FOR WINTER

*D*EAR Lord of hope,
Be close to me through the Winter months,
When days are shorter and darker,
Let me feel Your presence.
When winds blow stronger and colder,
Let Your love warm and comfort me.
Keep me safe in my going out
And my coming in.
Let me always remember —
I never walk alone.

Iris Hesselden.

TUESDAY—DECEMBER 5.

FUCHSIAS, rhododendrons, roses and many other flowers were all growing together, creating a delightful scent. I saw this beautiful sight in Eire in the hedgerows as I walked along, admiring the breathtaking views. The soil is stony and rocky, and you wonder how such a miracle can happen.

Later, as I was thinking about it all, I realised how some people can appear forbidding but like the flowers in the hedgerows growing in poor soil, there is often something worthwhile hiding behind the façade if we remember to look for it.

WEDNESDAY—DECEMBER 6.

I ALWAYS admire the story of Sarah Breedlove whose parents were slaves in America in the 19th century. She was orphaned at six, married at 14, and widowed at 20. For many years she worked as a washerwoman, struggling to support herself and her little daughter.

Then she had an idea! It was a recipe for a hair treatment. She worked away in her wash tub with soaps and ointments until at last she found a formula which would result in beautiful soft, shiny hair.

Moving to Colorado she marketed her "Brilliantine" as she'd called it. Sales flourished, and Madame Walker, as she was then known after marrying again, became well respected.

Everyone knew of her Brilliantine, but she was best known for her contributions to the community. She worked very hard and gave generously to help the underprivileged — and encouraged others to follow her example. A great deal of her fortune later went towards carrying on her good works.

So now, when you comb your hair, spare a thought for this woman who gave all of her life for others.

THURSDAY—DECEMBER 7.

LOVE one another, be kind and patient and the world will be a better place.

When the world is dark and gloomy, stand on tip-toe, and reach out to the light.

THE FRIENDSHIP BOOK

FRIDAY—DECEMBER 8.

I WONDER if you know these lines? They can be found at the end of George Du Maurier's novel "Trilby" and I thought you would appreciate them. Their wisdom is as true today, as when they were published in 1894.

A little work, a little play
  To keep us going — and so good day!
A little warmth, a little light
  Of love's bestowing — and so good night!
A little fun to match the sorrow
  Of each day's growing — and so good morrow!
A little trust that when we die
  We reap our sowing! And so — goodbye.

SATURDAY—DECEMBER 9.

I ONCE read about a gentleman who worked at a disposal plant in Glasgow and was known to many disadvantaged children as the Toyman.

Dave Wallace was his name and he said that it amazed him what folk threw away — toys, games, old annuals and cuddly toys. He retrieved them, then gave them a good wash, a lick of paint or a spot of glue so that they were quite usable again. For mechanical faults, he usually found an expert at the depot who could do the neccessary repairs. When he had enough gifts, they were delivered to a resource centre or a toy library.

"Waste not, want not," was a saying my older relatives used a lot when I was young, and Dave Wallace certainly put this adage into practice for a deserving cause.

SUNDAY—DECEMBER 10.

HOW great are his signs! and how mighty are his wonders! his kingdom is an everlasting kingdom, and his dominion is from generation to generation.

Daniel 4:3

MONDAY—DECEMBER 11.

IT was hard work that afternoon trudging the last few steps home, for I had caught a cold and was feeling like a piece of chewed string, when Roger, a neighbour, overtook me. "What an awful day!" he said, and then sneezed. I agreed, and out came my handkerchief again.

"Oh, you've got a cold, too," remarked Roger. "Well, I'm going home to do three things."

"And what are they?" I asked.

"First, a hot bath, and then a warm bed," came the reply. "And the third?" I prompted.

Roger sneezed again, and pulled his scarf more tightly round his neck. "I'm going to thank God I've gone so long this freezing Winter without a cold." He chuckled. "Bye, Francis!"

We parted, and the thought came to me — there goes a Christian with a cold in his head but a fire in his heart! And, do you know, I somehow began to feel better . . .

TUESDAY—DECEMBER 12.

"**W**HAT do we live for if it is not to make life less difficult for each other?"

Mary Anne Evans (George Eliot).

WEDNESDAY—DECEMBER 13.

HELPING HANDS

*A*S you tread life's highway,
  Face it with a smile,
*Do not hesitate to help
  The lame dog o'er the stile.*

*To each and every one of us
  A chance is daily given
To make this world for someone
  A little more like Heaven.*

Maurice Fleming.

THURSDAY—DECEMBER 14.

A FRIEND called to see the Lady of the House and me one day, and we began to talk about old times. It reminded me of these words by Oliver Goldsmith: "I love everything old; old friends, old times, old manners, old wine".

I recited them to Iris and she looked at me with a twinkle in her eye. "That's lovely, Francis," she said, "but I'll let you into a little secret. I love anything new!"

Her smile broadened as she went on, "A new tablet of soap. A new writing pad. Even a new packet of biscuits." We all laughed as she explained that she was on her way to pick up new holiday brochures.

After Iris left, we thought about her zest for life and wondered if her love of all things new had anything to do with it. After all, she is only eighty years young and has a lot of living still to do!

THE FRIENDSHIP BOOK

FRIDAY—DECEMBER 15.

AT this time of year I love to walk along our road at twilight, for then I can be sure that the Christmas tree lights have been switched on. Sometimes, too, there are twinkling lights round windows and doors, and trees in gardens may be festooned with coloured lamps.

These decorations never fail to bring pleasure, because they have been displayed more for the benefit of passers-by than that of the owners.

So, at this season of goodwill, the lights serve as a reminder to me that people everywhere are uniting to celebrate the birth of Jesus, who came to bring light into a dark world and to restore peace and justice to all mankind.

May you know the true blessings of Christmas.

SATURDAY—DECEMBER 16.

THERE'S another lady in my life,
And truthfully I'll say
She's captured my affections
In the most uncanny way.

It's true that I'm much older,
But I have to make the claim
Our relationship is special,
And I hope she feels the same.

Before the tongues start wagging,
The truth must now be told —
That lady's my granddaughter,
And she's only three months old!
J. M. Robertson.

SUNDAY—DECEMBER 17.

AND he took them up in his arms, put his hands upon them, and blessed them.

Mark 10:16

MONDAY—DECEMBER 18.

OUR friend, Harriet, came to tell us about her grandson's wedding, which she had hugely enjoyed. It brought back memories of her own wedding, more than 60 years before and also of her one-night only honeymoon.

She chuckled as she recalled carrying, on the train, a brown paper parcel tied with string. A suitcase would have been an unnecessary extravagance.

"No-one could have been happier," she told us. "And it was the start of a simply wonderful married life. I hope my grandson and his wife will be equally happy."

We both found this a rather touching story. However, the smile on Harriet's face made us realise the details were unimportant. What is important, though, was how she and her husband had found the main ingredient for marriage and for life itself — true love. Uncomplicated, unselfish and absolutely priceless.

What more could anyone wish for?

TUESDAY—DECEMBER 19.

IT is a joy to meet up with a good friend. It makes the glad heart even lighter, and can even make a dull day seem the brighter!

SHINING GLORY

WEDNESDAY—DECEMBER 20.

THE Lady Of The House had been baking, and was taking particular care over decorating a tasty-looking walnut cake.

"I'm afraid this isn't for us, Francis," she explained. "I've made it for Amy — she's been ill, you know — so for the first time ever she's allowing me to help."

We both laughed, for I knew exactly what she meant. Amy is always the first to offer assistance to others, but is so reluctant to receive help herself. This is a pity for, admirable as it is to give, sometimes it's just as important to receive — to allow other people their own turn at being generous.

As the Lady of the House smilingly pointed out, "Everybody likes to feel needed!"

THURSDAY—DECEMBER 21.

IT is nearly Christmas, and I have chosen a verse for you from my scrapbook. I wonder if you know these lines by the American poet Longfellow? They are from "Christmas Bells".

I heard the bells on Christmas Day
Their old familiar carols play,
And wild and sweet
The words repeat
Of peace on earth, goodwill to men.

Peace on earth, goodwill to men — isn't that what Christmas is all about? I wish you a Christmas both happy and peaceful!

FRIDAY—DECEMBER 22.

MEMORIES are golden gifts. Store safely, handle carefully and they will never tarnish.

SATURDAY—DECEMBER 23.

A FRIEND told us about 13-year-old Philip, a member of her village church choir and also a paper boy. Daily he delivered to Rose Cottage, a mile or so outside the village, where the elderly Miss Mitchell lived. She mentioned that the choir never got as far as her with their Christmas serenading.

"They will," Philip assured her.

That Christmas Eve the choir toured the village, completing their round at the usual spot.

"What about Rose Cottage?" Philip asked.

"Sorry," he was told, "it's too far away."

The boy ran home, collected his bike and pedalled for all he was worth. In the dark outside Miss Mitchell's cottage, his treble voice pealed out the carols of seasonal cheer. The door opened and, amazed and delighted, the old lady stood listening to the boy who had kept his word.

Young Philip had shown that he understood the true meaning of Christmas.

SUNDAY—DECEMBER 24.

AND the angel said unto them, Fear not: for behold, I bring you good tidings of great joy, which shall be to all people.

Luke 2:10

MONDAY—DECEMBER 25.

THE Lady of the House and I had gone through all the usual preparations for Christmas — the present buying and wrapping; we had attended the junior school's nativity play; we had enjoyed the early morning excitement of Christmas morning; finally, we had arrived at church for the morning service.

Everything seemed to be as usual, except that as the service proceeded a living tableau was formed at the front. Quietly and reverently a first-time young mother dressed as Mary placed her own very small baby into the manger.

It was at this point that I heard an awed and hushed whisper beside me say, "It's a real baby! Look, it's real!"

Suddenly, the whole familiar "story" was real — in that child's look of wonder I saw the first glimpse of true understanding.

Thinking about it afterwards, another thought came to me — every newborn child brings the message that God has not despaired of man.

TUESDAY—DECEMBER 26.

THE girl in the shoe shop obviously loved her job. "I look at it this way," she told me. "Every time I sell a pair of shoes, I'm giving someone a fresh start. I like to think all my customers make a new beginning with the shoes I've sold them."

Can you wonder I walked out with a spring in my step that wasn't there before?

WHITE
CHRISTMAS

WEDNESDAY—DECEMBER 27.

THE Lady of the House and I have a neighbour who lost her sight in an accident some years ago. She is a very independent person and we greatly admire her spirit. We wondered what to choose as a present for Lorna one Christmas. Suddenly the Lady of the House had an idea.

"You know, Francis," she said, "Lorna uses her radio-cassette player every day without fail. Why not make a tape of her favourite verses and some music?"

I thought it was an excellent suggestion and together we put together a collection of poems and rounded it all off with some cheerful music. Later we received a phone call from Lorna. She was delighted with her gift, she said, and would play the tape often.

This surely proves that it is not the most expensive gift which gives the greatest pleasure.

THURSDAY—DECEMBER 28.

PASSERS-BY often stop to admire old Adam's garden with its lovely flowerbeds which seem to have something blooming all year round. He's always pleased to see folk looking over the hedge.

"Well, it's like this, Francis," he says. "I can't write a book, compose a tune or paint a picture — but if my garden gives others pleasure, then I'm a happy man!"

He deserves to be.

FRIDAY—DECEMBER 29.

SOME people may regret that they had no opportunity to attend further education after leaving school, and perhaps some cannot readily take part in adult education.

Here the experience of Howard Spring, the author of "Fame Is The Spur", can be invaluable. In his autobiography he wrote of his early days as a reporter in Bradford. He explained how he had noted John Masefield's observation that one book leads to another, and each can widen the reader's interests and knowledge of life.

Many people have discovered this and it certainly enriches their lives. I started following Howard Spring's advice years ago!

SATURDAY—DECEMBER 30.

AS the old year ends, and we look forward to a new one, let us think about these words of Sir William Blackstone, the 18th-century jurist and legal writer: "Mankind will not be reasoned out of the feelings of humanity".

Cheerful and inspiring, with their belief in human goodness, the truth of the words, I am sure, will be proved over and over again in the coming New Year, which I hope will be a happy and fulfilling one for you all.

SUNDAY—DECEMBER 31.

FINALLY, my brethren, be strong in the Lord, and in the power of his might.

Ephesians 6:10

The Photographs

BEACH BEACON — *Hale Lighthouse, Cheshire.*
AFTER EIGHT . . . — *Albert Dock, Liverpool.*
NATURE'S SCULPTURE — *Loch Rannoch, Perthshire.*
COLUMBA'S ISLE — *Iona Abbey.*
COOL CASCADE — *Buachaille Etive Mhor, Argyll.*
KEELS AND CREELS — *Elie Harbour, Fife.*
BRIGHTON BELLE — *The Royal Pavilion, Brighton.*
HARBOUR HAVEN — *Whitby Harbour.*
EYES TO THE HILLS — *Llyn Gwynant, Snowdonia.*
SUNSET SYMPHONY — *Skye from Mallaig.*
MASTS AND MOUNTAINS — *Plockton, Wester Ross.*
OPEN HOUSE — *Fortingall, Perthshire.*
FOOTPRINTS IN THE SAND — *Harris, Outer Hebrides.*
SHELTER FROM THE STORM — *St Mary's, Isles of Scilly.*
PERFECT PEACE — *Sheffield Park House, East Sussex.*
MY SPECIAL PLACE — *Rydal Water, Lake District.*
HEAVEN SCENT — *Leuchars, Fife.*
HEART TO HEART — *Memorial Park, York.*
CUT AND DRIED — *Cranham, Gloucestershire.*
STATELY SPLENDOUR — *Wakehurst Place, Sussex.*
SUNSET SONG — *West Tarbert Loch, Kintyre.*
HAPPY WANDERERS — *Cumbria.*
CAPITAL COLOUR — *Edinburgh Castle.*
SEASON'S GREETINGS — *Chester.*
SHINING GLORY — *Loch Lomond from Ardlui.*
WHITE CHRISTMAS — *Winter in Strathglass, Inverness-shire.*

ACKNOWLEDGEMENTS: **Ivan J. Belcher;** Masts And Mountains, My Special Place. **Paul Felix;** Shelter From The Storm, Cut And Dried. **V. K. Guy;** Mother Knows Best, Happy Wanderers. **Dennis Hardley;** Columba's Isle, Beach Beacon, After Eight . . ., Nature's Sculpture, Cool Cascade, Keels And Creels, Brighton Belle, Harbour Haven, Open House, Footprints In The Sand, Perfect Peace, Heaven Scent, Heart To Heart, Season's Greetings, Shining Glory. **Irene Lawson;** Capital Colour. **Duncan McEwan;** White Christmas. **Clifford Robinson;** New Beginnings. **Willie Shand;** Sunset Symphony. **Andrew Taylor;** Stocking Up. **Iain White;** Sunset Song. **Andy Williams;** Silver Webbing, Eyes To The Hills, Stately Splendour.

Printed and Published by D. C. Thomson & Co., Ltd.,
185 Fleet Street, London EC4A 2HS.
© D. C. Thomson & Co., Ltd., 1999   **ISBN** 0-85116-710-1